Chaim Perelman

RHETORIC IN THE MODERN ERA

Arthur E. Walzer and Edward Schiappa, Editors

The goal of the series "Rhetoric in the Modern Era" is to prompt and sponsor book-length treatments of important rhetorical theorists and of philosophers and literary theorists who make substantial contributions to our understanding of language and rhetoric. In some cases, a book in this series is the first book-length treatment of the figure; in others, a book in the series is the first to examine a philosopher or theorist from the perspective of rhetorical theory.

The intended audience for books in the series are nonspecialists—graduate students coming to the study of a theorist for the first time and professors broadly interested in the rhetorical tradition. The series books are comprehensive introductions—comprehensive in the sense that they provide brief biographies, descriptions of the intellectual milieu, and discussions of the major scholarship on the figure as context for a detailed examination of the figure's contribution to rhetorical theory or history.

We envision these as the first books on their subject, not the last. While books in the series may exceed these modest aims, their focus is on achieving them. A complete list of the books in the series can be found at the end of this volume.

Chaim Perelman

❄

ALAN G. GROSS
AND
RAY D. DEARIN

SOUTHERN ILLINOIS UNIVERSITY PRESS
CARBONDALE AND EDWARDSVILLE

First edition published by State University of New York Press 2003

Printed in the United States of America

13 12 11 10 4 3 2 1

Library of Congress Cataloging-in-Publication Data

Gross, Alan G.
Chaim Perelman / Alan G. Gross and Ray D. Dearin.
p. cm. — (Rhetoric in the modern era series)
Includes bibliographical references and index.
ISBN-13: 978-0-8093-3022-5 (pbk. : alk. paper)
ISBN-10: 0-8093-3022-9 (pbk. : alk. paper)
ISBN-13: 978-0-8093-8621-5 (ebook)
ISBN-10: 0-8093-8621-6 (ebook)
1. Perelman, Chaïm. 2. Reasoning—History—20th century. 3. Rhetoric—History—20th century. 4. Logic, Modern—20th century. I. Dearin, Ray D., 1941– II. Title.
B4165.P474G76 2010
199'.493—DC22 2010007509

The paper used in this publication meets the minimum requirements of American National Standard for Information Sciences—Permanence of Paper for Printed Library Materials, ANSI Z39.48-1992. ♾

To James Clifford Nilsen: In Memoriam
A Good Man and the Best of Friends
—Alan Gross

To my parents,
James Burien Dearin and Thelma Pauline Dearin,
whose love and support have meant everything to me
—Ray Dearin

Contents

Preface

For each of us, Perelman has been a central figure, hovering steadily over our scholarly work, our excursions into rhetorical theory and rhetorical criticism. We hope that this short book helps others also see the inspirational importance of his achievement. Still, there is no getting away from the fact that *The New Rhetoric* is difficult to read, a task made even more difficult for American audiences because virtually all its examples and illustrations are from a literature in a foreign language. We have addressed this latter problem by drawing our examples largely from American sources, mostly from the work of Abraham Lincoln. But stubborn expository difficulties remain. Moreover, Perelman's later attempts to achieve clarity, in *The Realm of Rhetoric*, and numerous shorter articles, are equally puzzling. Consequently, some of Perelman's best ideas are virtually buried in a very long work, and therefore largely lost even to the most careful readers. In addition, on such central issues as the relationship between rhetoric and philosophy Perelman remains maddeningly obscure. While there has been some useful exegesis in English, most of it merely perpetuates misunderstandings that stem from superficial acquaintance; the few articles that might be helpful are nestled nearly beyond recovery in dusty and largely unread periodical volumes.

This expository feebleness would not matter if Perelman were not, in our opinion, one of Aristotle's most important heirs; if he did not develop the Master's ideas in ways that match in fruitfulness the work of Kenneth Burke, one of the most important maverick Aristotelians. We think it is not incidental to Perelman's interest in rhetoric, moreover, that he was, like Aristotle, a philosopher deeply concerned with the idea of justice. In our view, the most significant tenet of *The New Rhetoric* concerns the centrality of rhetoric in a world in which human freedom is also central: "Only an existence of an argumentation that is neither compelling nor arbitrary can give meaning to human freedom" (514).

While we are conscious of Perelman's considerable merits, we are not blind, we think, to his limitations. He renovates and refurbishes each of the key Aristotelian components of rhetoric—invention, style, and arrangement. In addition, he adds insight to insight in his discussion of two of the Aristotelian proofs: ethos, from the character of the speaker, and logos, from the lines of reasoning of the speech. But he is almost entirely silent on pathos, that is, proofs that derive from the emotional state of the audience. In this, he seems a true heir of the Enlightenment, distrustful of emotional proofs as inimical to reason and rationality. In recent decades, however, in the work of such scholars as Martha Nussbaum (from classics), Antonio Damasio (from neurophysiology), and Jon Elster (from political theory), we have become aware that the emotions have a rational component: in certain situations at least, we require the emotions in order to act reasonably. This scholarship has also reminded us that Aristotle's theory of the emotions, enunciated in the *Rhetoric*, is deeply cognitive, and that in the *Ethics* Aristotle asserts, as he should, that the emotions are central to ethics: there are some things at which we ought to be angry. Can it be rational to maintain our equanimity when what we hold dear is insulted and traduced, or when the guilty go free, and the innocent are slaughtered?

There is another, graver fault that can be imputed to Perelman. If human freedom depends, as he seems to imply, on a free exchange of views in the public sphere, why does he theorize almost exclusively about the arguments that people make rather than about the process of arguing? On this topic, his work seems to have been far outdistanced by Jürgen Habermas, a scholar who has devoted his maturity to the elaboration of a theory of communicative action, and to its application to the crucial arenas of ethics and the law. An excerpt from *Between Facts and Norms* gives the flavor of Habermas's work:

> A legal order is legitimate to the extent that it equally secures the co-original private and political autonomy of its citizens; at the same time, however, it *owes* its legitimacy to the forms of communication in which alone this autonomy can express and prove itself. In the final analysis, the legitimacy of law depends on the undistorted forms of public communication and indirectly on the communicational infrastructure of the private sphere as well. This is the key to a proceduralist understanding of law. (409)

Clearly rhetorical critics need a theory of this sort if their work is not to be reduced to a knack in Plato's pejorative sense; but just as clearly theory at this level of relentless abstraction has no purchase whatever when it comes to the elucidation of actual texts. In this arena, Perelman and his collaborator, Lucie Olbrechts-Tyteca, still reign supreme. Theirs is a microanalysis of arguments, one that is endlessly suggestive of ways of analyzing texts at the level of the word and phrase, of the arrangement of parts, and of the structure of arguments.

One last fault of Perelman's must be mentioned. For a man so deeply imbued with a sense of justice, he may nevertheless have done an injustice to his long-term collaborator, Lucie Olbrechts-Tyteca, by not specifying her role in the creation of *The New Rhetoric*. (Of course, she could have spoken up also.) The only clue Perelman has left us is the placement of her name second on the original title page in reduced type. What was Madame Olbrechts-Tyteca's actual role as co-author of *The New Rhetoric*? Taking her cue from Perelman's professional identity, and from an examination of Olbrechts-Tyteca's independent works, Barbara Warnick gives the philosophical sections to Perelman, the elaborate exemplifications to his co-author. This is fair enough, but it leaves unattributed some of the most interesting sections of *The New Rhetoric*, those in which the argumentative implications of style and arrangement are discussed. It also leaves unattributed the central insight that works of philosophy depend fundamentally on the rhetorical device of dissociation. In these matters, who did what? Without additional evidence, we must withhold judgment.

In our exposition of the Belgians' ideas, we have chosen not to follow the order of *The New Rhetoric*, which moves from the framework of argument on to its starting points and techniques. We find that this order tends to obscure their most interesting ideas in a mass of detail. Instead, after brief biography, we focus on the philosophical foundations of their rhetorical theory. At this point, we switch to the theory itself: We attempt to give the reader a clear picture of their central concept—a concept central to any rhetorical theory—that of audience. After that exposition, in separate chapters, we take up three crucial Perelmanian ways of arguing: 1) quasilogically, 2) from the structure of reality, and 3) from the establishment of the structure of reality. Next, we take up the vexed question of the relation of rhetoric to truth, a troubling question since Plato first broached it. We show that a fourth Perelmanian way of arguing, dissociation, deals adequately with this question, at least to the satisfaction of the Belgian co-authors. In the next two chapters, we present two issues the tradition has neglected, but which the Belgians feature: the role of arrangement and of the figures in argument. In a final chapter we focus on what we regard as the keystone in the Perelmanian rhetorical arch: the concept of presence. We try to make sense of this concept within the framework of Perelmanian philosophy and to extend it in a way that we hope the Belgians would find acceptable. Finally, we include a selective bibliography. (A bibliography complete as of 1979 was published in the memorial issue of the *Revue Internationale de Philosophie:* 33, 1979.)

CHAPTER 1

Perelman's Life and Influence

Chaim Perelman was born May 20, 1912, in Warsaw, Poland, the son of Abraham and Lea (Garbownik) Perelman.[1] His father was a diamond merchant who moved his family to Antwerp, Belgium, in 1925, where the young immigrant entered the secondary school system. During his last year of high school, he was exposed to a course called the "Elements of Rhetoric," in which the final examination required him to master the contents of a small, two-part handbook. One section dealt with patterns of logic known as syllogisms, the other with language devices such as tropes and figures of speech. Young Perelman wondered what possible connection professors of rhetoric could see between these two topics.

After completing his secondary education, Perelman enrolled at the Free University of Brussels, an institution where he would remain, except for visiting professorships abroad, for the rest of his life. Among the professors who influenced Perelman at Brussels was Eugène Dupréel, the prominent sociologist whose *Traité de Morale* argued forcefully that social groupings result from a confluence of shared values, and that moral standards reflect the way a society evaluates specific actions. Under Dupréel's tutelage, Perelman began to explore a conundrum that had plagued philosophers for centuries: How does one arrive at a logical basis for rendering value judgments? Perelman's first published article, written when he was 19 years old, mirrored the assumptions of logical positivism; it stressed the futility of trying to settle disputes regarding values ("Esquisse"). A second article dealing with the philosophical ideas of his mentor Dupréel followed the next year. Then, when he was still only 21, Perelman published two seminal essays: an analysis of the social status of truth-judgments ("Le Statut Social") and a systematic examination of the place of arbitrary elements in a theory of knowledge

("De l'Arbitraire"). The seeds of a brilliant academic career were already germinating when he was awarded a doctorate in law in 1934 and a second doctorate in philosophy in 1938.

On January 13, 1935, Perelman married Felicie (Fela) Liwer. Their lifelong union produced one child, a daughter, Noémi Perelman Mattis, who followed in her father's footsteps, earning two doctorates, a J.D. and a Ph.D. in psychology.

In 1938 Perelman was appointed as a lecturer on the Faculty of Philosophy and Letters at Brussels. On November 14 of that year he successfully defended his doctoral dissertation on Gottlob Frege, a nineteenth-century German mathematician who had conducted a systematic study of the patterns of reasoning used by mathematicians.

For the most part, Perelman's writings at the end of the 1930s remained strongly anchored in the intellectual currents of that era: Cartesian rationalism, logical positivism, and empiricism. His analysis of several logical paradoxes and antinomies in law had shaken his faith in these doctrines, but his attachments to the orthodoxy of his age had not been completely severed. In a 1940 article he described resemblances between scientific and philosophical reasoning: "The philosophical method has the same logical structure as that of science. It consists of deducing from certain principles and from certain definitions . . . a set of consequences, and of comparing, as far as possible, these consequences with the facts" ("Une Conception" 46). So long as facts, definitions, and logical inferences were at issue, the tenets of positivism seemed sound, but what should be done about values? Must all philosophical discussions involving values be dismissed as baseless in logic, and therefore without any foundation in reason itself?

The idea that basic values are totally impervious to logical argument was unquestioned by logicians and epistemologists in the Europe of 1940. That same year, Albert Einstein, a theoretical physicist, spoke for virtually the whole intellectual community when he said, "I know that it is a hopeless undertaking to debate about fundamental value judgments. For instance, if someone approves, as a goal, the extirpation of the human race from the earth, one cannot refute such a viewpoint on rational grounds" (31). The banishment of ultimate values from all rational deliberation had pernicious consequences, however, and history soon intruded into the lofty philosophizing of the young man who had embarked upon such a promising career at the University of Brussels. Certain values were, in fact, being espoused which threatened to extirpate Einstein's—and Perelman's—own race from the face of the earth. These values, moreover, were being ruthlessly translated into public policies and enforced by the military power of a modern political state.

When the German occupation of Belgium began, Perelman and three other Jewish faculty members at the University of Brussels came under the subjection of the anti-Semitic Nuremberg laws. They were asked by the rector of the university to resign, but refused as a matter of conscience. They finally agreed not to teach but did not sever their connection with the university (Gérard-Libois 462). For the duration of the war, Perelman continued to receive his salary through an intermediary (Steinberg, I, 112).

Interviewed for an oral history project twenty years after the war, Perelman recalled that "the intensification of the anti-Jewish measures gave the signal to various movements of the Jewish resistance which soon united in their efforts" (I, 69–70; interview). Perelman participated in the resistance as a founding member of the Comité de Défense des Juifs (C. D. J.), which was created under the aegis of the Independence Front. Operating under the *nom de guerre* "Dumont," he helped the C. D. J. rescue thousands of Jews from death at the hands of the Nazis. He also helped to publish and distribute underground newspapers.

Perelman moved around Belgium with relative ease during the occupation. He was deputy chief, and later chief, of the adult service of the Association des Juifs en Belgique (A. J. B.), the organization charged with the management of Jewish life under the German authorities. Although his work involved cooperation with the Nazis, a complicity that included, of course, the deportation of thousands to the death camps, Perelman was not a collaborator; he used his position as a cover for his secret activities designed to aid his fellow Jews. To be sure, he could not escape "the undeniable logic of a system created by the occupying power and under the vigilant surveillance of an SS officer in charge of Jewish affairs" (I, 52). Nevertheless, he used his official position to divert ration stamps and packages of food and supplies to those in hiding. He also supplied them with money obtained from the American Jewish Joint Distribution Committee and channeled through Switzerland (I, 95–96; interview). These underground activities were extremely dangerous, but Perelman was arrested only once—by the Currency Police, not the Gestapo—on a matter unrelated to his clandestine work in behalf of the Jews. He was held for two days and released (I, 114). Fela Perelman was also involved in the resistance movement. She ran a school for Jewish children that became a center to hide them from the Nazis and place them in Catholic homes (I, 172).

The Perelmans were not partisans or resistance fighters but were intelligent, capable managers of an underground network designed to rescue Jewish adults and children from deportation and death.

In his postwar reminiscences, Perelman tended to gloss over differences among the various Jewish factions of the Belgian underground. The Perelmans had no sympathy for the communists, and the communists wasted little sympathy on them, though they did work together. Perelman's tendency to make the past look rosier than it was is reflected in his comments in 1979 concerning the role of non-Jewish Belgians in the rescue of Jews. Perelman said that "if the resistance to the Occupation could be measured in Western Europe by the percentage of the Jewish population saved from deportation, it is Belgium, after Denmark that merits second place." Commenting on this view, Maxime Steinberg says that the professor ignored the case of France, as well as the facts themselves. "In effect," Perelman claimed, "nearly half of the Jews were able to escape deportation and this thanks essentially to the active collaboration of the Belgian people." To this assertion, Steinberg responds that the evidence for such active collaboration is nonexistent (I, 257–258). Whatever the case, nearly 29,000 Jews lost their lives in the camps, about 44 percent of the Jewish population of Belgium (II, 259). If it had not been for the efforts of the resistance, Perelman believed the number would have been 47,000 (interview).

As the Germans retreated from Belgium and the war in Europe came to an end, Chaim Perelman resumed his brilliant academic career, becoming the youngest full professor in the history of the University of Brussels (Mattis). Before we consider his remarkable burst of intellectual activity in the postwar years, however, it is fitting to acknowledge his many contributions to the educational and cultural affairs of Israel. In July, 1946, before the new Jewish state was founded in Palestine, Chaim and Fela Perelman organized the embarkation from Antwerp of a boat full of "illegal" immigrants bound for Palestine. When Israel became an independent nation, Perelman knew many of its leading figures, from prime ministers such as David Ben-Gurion and Golda Meier to Teddy Kollek, the mayor of Jerusalem. He served on the board of governors of Hebrew University and was a founding member of the Belgian Friends of that institution. He presided over the Action Committee for Israel, the Information and Documentation Center on the Middle East, and the Tribute Committee to Belgian Rescuers. In 1955, he established the Menoah Association, which held conferences and published a monthly newspaper devoted to maintaining links between Jewish life in Belgium and Israel.

These activities reflected Perelman's ethnic and cultural heritage as a Jew. He had been forced to wear the yellow Star of David and had seen his fellow Jews sent to their death. For him, being a Jew was an inescapable part of his identity. Throughout his life, however, both before and after the war, Perelman remained an intellectual product of European humanism, a secular or cosmopolitan Jew whose Zionist aspirations were totally void of religious overtones. As Mieczyslaw Maneli, a close friend, described Perelman's faith, "He very consistently rejects any theology or earthly or heavenly salvation, any monism of values, any absolutistic interpretations of human needs and forms of freedom. Any form of theology is unacceptable to him" (1986, 354–355). Fela Perelman's religious ties to Judaism were stronger than her husband's. One of her grandfathers had been the Grand Rabbi of Lodj, Poland. Like her husband, though, she pursued a secular education and became a scholar in her own right. Among other achievements, she earned a doctorate in history and wrote a book comparing the Polish and Belgian revolutions (Mattis *Tzedek* 3).

By the time Brussels was liberated on September 3, 1944, Perelman had already resumed his philosophical investigations. He had undertaken an exhaustive analysis of the idea of *justice*, a "confused notion," as he would later call it. For centuries philosophers and politicians had wrangled incessantly over the varying meanings attached to the word "justice," and no existing paradigm of reason seemed capable of settling these disputes. The results of Perelman's investigation were published in an 84-page treatise entitled *De la Justice* (1945). In it, he formulated for the first time a "rule of justice," which he posited as the underlying basis of *all rational activity*. As we shall see in Chapter 2, the judicial model of reasoning that resulted from this study became a foundational element in his entire philosophical enterprise.

In Perelman's early postwar writings, the inadequacies of rationalism and logical positivism stood out in stark relief. The canons of logic bequeathed by the past were shown to be irrelevant and ineffectual in a world that had gone mad. During the war, the young philosopher had witnessed the banality of evil and the fickleness of fortune; now he struggled with the notions of free will and human action. He wondered whether any rational basis could possibly be found for the choices humans have to make every day, especially when these decisions cannot be linked to necessity or self-evidence. Are such judgments entirely whimsical, capricious, and arbitrary? As he grappled with these questions, Perelman, whose title was professor of law, logic, and metaphysics, pursued an eclectic research agenda that transcended existing academic disciplines; his prolific writings appeared in philosophical reviews, sociological journals, conference proceedings in ethics and logic, and in publications devoted to international law and the search for world peace.

Perelman was not a reclusive scholar who confined himself to his study for extended periods of introspection. Rather, he was a voluble conversationalist, a gregarious and engaging guest at social gatherings of all kinds. He enjoyed talking about his latest ideas with anyone who would listen, and a coterie of attentive listeners often collected around him at parties and receptions (Mattis). In 1948, when he was 36, a woman thirteen years his senior was drawn into his circle and became one of his most devoted listeners.

At 49 years of age, Madame Lucie Olbrechts-Tyteca became an unlikely collaborator with Perelman on a project that would consume a decade of feverish intellectual activity on his part—and a decade of tedious, painstaking effort on hers. Lucie Tyteca had been born in 1899 into one of Brussels' most prominent families. She was the daughter and only child of the psychiatrist who founded the Tyteca Institute of Neuropsychiatry. Like most women of means in Belgium during that era, she did not pursue a professional career, although her inquisitive mind led her to obtain a *license*, or four-year degree, from Brussels University. Her education was broadly based in literature and the social sciences. Unlike Perelman, for whom Eugène Dupréel was a close mentor, Lucie Tyteca probably encountered the eminent sociologist as a student in one his large lecture courses to several hundred students (Mattis). She also studied economics and psychology, and learned to use statistical research methods (Olbrechts-Tyteca 3). Her education in the liberal arts and sciences complemented Perelman's philosophical and legal training. Her temperament and private circumstances made her an ideal research associate.

Lucie Tyteca was married to Raymond Olbrechts, a professor of statistics in the business school at Brussels, who was eleven years older than she was. As Perelman's daughter remembers her as a family friend, "She had no children, hardly any family, and very little social life. Her husband was an introvert and spent long hours in his study. She was painfully shy, not the kind to venture anywhere on her own. She never learned to drive a car. In 1948 she was 49 years old, a lady of leisure with not much to occupy herself. She read a lot" (Mattis). Evidently the reclusive Mme. Olbrechts did attend enough social affairs to become fascinated by the charismatic young philosopher, for she was soon drawn into his orbit. Hearing him talk excitedly about a research project he had in mind, she volunteered to assist him.

By the time Perelman met Olbrechts-Tyteca, he had already formulated certain philosophical presuppositions, which we shall examine in Chapter 2.

For now, it is sufficient to note that Perelman's rather grandiose philosophic mission had also taken shape by the late 1940s. As expressed by Max Loreau, that goal was "*to produce an instrument capable of achieving in the realm of values results exactly analogous to those pursued by analytical reasoning in the domain of the exact sciences*" (456). Stated succinctly, Perelman sought to discover a "logic of value judgments" applicable to the practical affairs of life where decisions have to be made every day without conclusive evidence or formally valid proofs.

Inspired by Frege's systematic approach to the collection and examination of evidence, and keeping in mind Dupréel's emphasis on the social role of values, Perelman and Olbrechts-Tyteca cast their net as widely as possible. They undertook a comprehensive analysis of the specimens of reasoning actually used by lawyers, philosophers, politicians, journalists, moralists, and others who try to "make a rule prevail" in situations where empirical evidence and formal logic cannot settle the issue. In the course of their investigations, the Belgians "rediscovered" the classical writings on rhetoric and dialectic, as exemplified by Aristotle's *Rhetoric* and *Topics*. The ancient treatises filled with syllogisms and figures of speech that had puzzled the young schoolboy in Antwerp now came to be seen in a new light, as elements of a lost and forgotten art, a mode of rationality scorned for centuries by philosophers enamored with the claims of Cartesian rationalism and logical positivism.

To say that rhetoric was in the 1940s a "forgotten" subject is to betray a Continental bias that Perelman later came to regard as provincial. He often pointed out that the word rhetoric was not mentioned in the *Encyclopedia of Philosophy* or in the French philosophical dictionary of Lalande. And in spite of his own recollection of having studied the "elements of rhetoric" in his youth, Perelman told the Wingspread Conference, a meeting of forty scholars to assess the future of rhetorical studies in January, 1970, that "the teaching of rhetoric has been struck from the programs of both high schools and universities in Europe for over fifty years" (Bitzer and Black 115). Seven years earlier, in her account of their joint project, Olbrechts-Tyteca made a frank confession: "Ch. Perelman and I were, at the beginning of our researches, about as ignorant of rhetoric as it was possible for a decent person [*honnête homme*] of the twentieth century to be" (3). Perelman later discovered that rhetorical studies had been carried on in American universities, chiefly in departments of speech, for several decades before he embarked upon his personal intellectual odyssey.

The raw materials amassed by Perelman and his colleague were culled from philosophical treatises, legal and historical writings, the sermons of La

Bruyère and Bossuet, the economic and political tracts of Bentham, Locke, and Mill, as well as fictional works—plays, poetry, and novels. Even the low-brow parody and satire found in popular humor magazines yielded up a plethora of argumentative devices, all of which had been catalogued centuries ago by the ancient Greeks and Romans. The person who actually "spent all her time reading away and gathering quotes on file cards" was Mme. Olbrechts. For his part, Perelman supplied the "theoretical armature" for the project (Mattis). He came to regard rhetoric and dialectic as parts of a unified whole, in which dialectic functions as the theoretical underpinning for a theory of nonformal reasoning (argumentation), whereas rhetoric constitutes a practical discipline that utilizes dialectical techniques to convince or to persuade. For a time, Perelman pondered whether to call the discipline he was seeking to "revive" dialectic or rhetoric. "I believe there should be no hesitation in calling it rhetoric," he finally concluded, "for our cultural milieu has for over a century identified dialectic with the conceptions of Hegel and Marx, and rhetoric is the only discipline traditionally concerned with an audience" (Bitzer 118). Hence the culmination of Perelman and Olbrechts-Tyteca's ten-year project came to be known as the "new rhetoric."

Perelman's personal commitment to the joint endeavor was intense and sustained, but it was far from single-minded. "Perelman's research went in several directions at once: informal logic, philosophy of law, reasoning in History, Rhetoric, etc.," recalls his daughter. "He had a full teaching load, held executive positions in national and International Professional societies as well as Jewish organizations. He had a busy social life and traveled extensively" (Mattis). Perelman continued to write about justice, humanism, freedom, democracy, and the nature of philosophical proofs. He produced an entire coursebook on logic for the Brussels University Press.

Perelman and Olbrechts-Tyteca's collaboration began to bear fruit in 1952 when they published a collection of essays entitled *Rhétorique et Philosophie*. With its suggestive subtitle, *Pour une Théorie de l'Argumentation en Philosophie*, the book explored the relationships between logic and rhetoric, freedom and responsibility, act and person in argumentation, and other topics related to the nature of "proof" in philosophical systems. Six years later, the vision of the authors expanded greatly beyond the initial probes and partial studies represented in this book. Their long research program finally culminated in the publication of a mammoth two-volume work bearing the audacious title *La Nouvelle Rhétorique: Traité de l'Argumentation* (Universitaires Presses de France, 1958). As a reward for her decade of unpaid labor, Perelman put Olbrechts' name on the book as a co-author, albeit in reverse alphabetical order and in reduced type. Afterwards he always insisted that both authors shared in the writing, although neither of them thought of the project as an equal collaboration (Mattis). As bulky as the treatise was, it contained only about a third of all the material Mme. Olbrechts had collected. Years later Perelman assisted her in putting together a book under her sole authorship, *Le Comique du Discours* (Brussels Press, 1974), utilizing material that had been trimmed from their major opus.

The English translation was published as *The New Rhetoric: A Treatise on Argumentation* by the University of Notre Dame Press in 1969. When it appeared, Perelman, who was already well established as a leading European philosopher, began to attract the attention of intellectuals and academics in a wide range of disciplines in the English-speaking countries. In the United States he had already aroused the curiosity of a small but growing clique of philosophers and legal theorists, as well as a handful of rhetorical scholars.

The first significant interchange between Perelman and American professors interested in his rhetorical ideas occurred in 1954, when Henry W. Johnstone, Jr., a young philosopher at Pennsylvania State University, reviewed *Rhétorique et Philosophie* for the journal *Philosophy and Phenomenological Research*. Johnstone had no interest in rhetoric but was intrigued by Perelman and Olbrechts-Tyteca's views on philosophical argumentation. For Johnstone, the term dialectic seemed to be a sufficient designator for what the Belgians had in mind. Perelman's response to Johnstone appeared in the same journal and a convivial relationship ensued. As Perelman and Olbrechts-Tyteca were putting the finishing touches on *The New Rhetoric*, Johnstone took a leave of absence and visited Belgium. "During his stay in Brussels," Perelman later recalled, "Johnstone told me nothing about the existence in the United States, and even in his own university . . . , of departments of speech interested in rhetoric" ("The New Rhetoric and the Rhetoricians" 188).

Perelman's introduction to the field of speech, which did not exist in Europe at that time, came in 1962 when he was invited to become a visiting distinguished professor at Penn State in the Departments of Philosophy and Speech. The invitation was from Johnstone and Robert T. Oliver, respective heads of the two departments. Significantly enough, it was Oliver who instigated the move to bring Perelman to the State College campus[2] ("The Way It Was" 121). Oliver had set out to build one of the premier speech departments in the United States, and his collaboration with the soundly "intellectual" philosophy department was a calculated means toward that end. The partnership between the Penn State rhetoricians and philosophers led to the founding of a new journal, *Philosophy and Rhetoric,* which first appeared in January, 1968, featuring an article by Perelman, who was also a member of its prestigious editorial board.

In 1963, the year after Perelman left Penn State, an entire issue of *Logique et Analyse* was devoted to the "new rhetoric." In it, Oliver, writing from the standpoint of an American rhetorical scholar, said of Perelman:

> If he is not so far removed from our theories as we had expected, neither is his thinking typical of that in our field. Rather, he now appears to us to stand midway between Philosophy and Speech as a kind of ideal ambassador: with a sympathetic understanding of the aims and purposes of each; able to look both ways and capable of interpreting the one to the other. It is a position of great strength from which, if his principles are widely and wisely adopted, both Philosophy and Speech may have much to profit. ("Philosophy and/or Persuasion" 580)

In 1965 Perelman's accessible paperback, *An Historical Introduction to Philosophical Thinking,* published in English by Random House, brought his name to a wider readership in the United States. That same year, the book review editor of the *Quarterly Journal of Speech,* Wayne E. Brockriede, asked Max Loreau, a colleague of Perelman's at Brussels, to write a lengthy review of Perelman's philosophical and rhetorical writings. For most American students of rhetoric, that essay—translated as "Rhetoric as the Logic of the Behavioral Sciences"—constituted their first encounter with the Belgian philosopher. Both Brockriede and Marie Hochmuth Nichols, who was the editor of the *QJS* at that time, deserve more credit than they have ever been given for introducing Chaim Perelman to the community of rhetorical scholars in the United States. In 1967 Nichols assigned a graduate student in her seminar in Modern Rhetorical Theory at the University of Illinois to report on the Loreau review. That student, one of the present authors, went on to write a *QJS* article (1969) and doctoral dissertation (1970) on Perelman (see Dearin, "Philosophical Basis"; "Chaim Perelman's Theory of Rhetoric"). By that time, Wayne Brockriede had succeeded Nichols as editor, and he also published Carroll C. Arnold's timely review of *The New Rhetoric* in 1970 ("Perelman's New Rhetoric").

By the middle of the 1970s, Perelman had been canonized in anthologies of contemporary rhetorical theory, textbooks, graduate theses, journal articles, and convention papers; he appeared alongside Kenneth Burke, I. A. Richards, and Richard Weaver, as a leading proponent of the so-called "New Rhetoric," a term that American scholars had been using for years before

Perelman and Olbrechts-Tyteca's treatise appeared in 1958. But the uniqueness of Perelman's contributions to the renewal of an ancient discipline could not be denied.

Not since Richard Whately's *Elements of Rhetoric* of 1828 had anyone elaborated a comprehensive system of rhetoric as the theory of argumentation to rival the one proffered by Perelman and Olbrechts-Tyteca. The vastness of the enterprise afforded Perelman plenty of opportunities to extend and refine his ideas. During the seventies as his reputation spread, he was in constant demand as a visiting lecturer and conference participant. He published condensed versions and spin-offs of the 1958 work: *Le Champ de l'Argumentation* (1970); *L'Empire Rhétorique* (1977), translated as *The Realm of Rhetoric* (1982); *Logique Juridique: Nouvelle Rhétorique* (1976); *The New Rhetoric and the Humanities* (1979); and *Justice, Law, and Argument* (1980). As these titles show, Perelman continued to view rhetoric as a nonformal logic, an everyday, working logic of the kind found, for example, in the courtroom. The juridical model of reasoning that emerged from his initial study of justice in 1944 continued to serve as the basis for his rhetorical thinking.

Actually, Perelman's legal training did more than supply grist for his rhetorical mill; it fueled an alternative career, one that paralleled his work as a logician, ethicist, and rhetorician. It would be possible, in fact, to write a substantial professional biography of Perelman as a legal theorist, beginning with his doctorate in law four years before his Ph.D. and extending throughout his lifetime, *without a single reference to his "specifically rhetorical" writings*. At the Free University of Brussels, he directed the National Center for Research in Logic, a branch of which he co-founded in 1971 as the Center for the Philosophy of Law. Under his direction, a stream of noteworthy books flowed forth, including *Fact and Law* (1961), *Antinomies in Law* (1965), *The Problem of Lacunae in Law* (1968), *The Rule of Law* (1974), *The Motivation of Decisions of Justice* (1978), *Proof in Law* (1981), and *Unsettled Ideas in Law* (1984). In addition, the center also published seven volumes of *Studies in Juridical Logic* from 1966 to 1978.[3] Perelman's own writings on juridical reasoning and related topics appeared in two books: *The Idea of Justice and the Problem of Argument* (1963) and *Justice* (1965). In 1966 he published an essay in the *National Law Forum* entitled "What the Philosopher May Learn from the Study of Law." In his last message to American rhetorical scholars, Perelman referred to that essay and ended on a cryptic note: "But it would require a substantial thesis in order to respond to the question, 'What the rhetorician may learn from the study of legal and judicial reasoning'" ("The New Rhetoric and the

Rhetoricians" 195). These words, published posthumously, hang in the air, leaving us to wonder how Perelman might have responded to that thesis.

By the beginning of the 1980s, Chaim Perelman had brought great renown to his adopted nation. His accolades included honorary degrees from the Universities of Florence, Jerusalem, and Montreal; he was made an officer of the Order of Leopold in 1955, a recipient of the Order of Merit in Italy in 1965, and a great officer of the Order of the Crown in 1978. Following the War, he had refused all medals for heroism in the resistance movement, declaring, "My heart was on fire. I simply picked up a pail of water to douse the flames" (Foss 120). Following an act of the Belgian legislature on December 5, 1983, in recognition of his philosophical and humanitarian accomplishments, Perelman finally acceded when King Baudouin of Belgium proclaimed him Baron Perelman. Fela received the corresponding title of Baroness Perelman.

Perelman continued to visit his devoted collaborator, Lucie Olbrechts-Tyteca, on at least a weekly basis. After nearly four decades, they "never let go of a quaint formality" (Mattis). When he visited her on January 21, 1984, he still addressed her as "Madame Olbrechts," and she addressed him as "Monsieur Perelman."

The next day, January 22, close friends of the Perelmans enjoyed a dinner with them in celebration of their recent elevation to the baronage. That evening Perelman died of a heart attack at his home in Brussels. On his tomb were inscribed words from Deuteronomy 16:20, which also appeared on his newly created coat of arms: "Justice, justice you shall pursue" (Mattis *Tzedek* 2).

CHAPTER 2

Philosophical Foundations

Every theory of rhetoric rests upon preconceptions about human behavior. Classical doctrines, markedly influenced by Aristotle, envisaged humans as rational beings, albeit with strong, sometimes decisive emotional proclivities; rhetoric itself was conceived to be an amoral art that could be used for good or ill, depending upon the motives of the persuader. Innovations in rhetorical theory have inevitably been associated with changing world views, as, for example, when Augustine appropriated Greek and Roman teachings and reinterpreted them in light of Christian pedagogical needs, or when the eighteenth-century Scottish cleric George Campbell incorporated contemporaneous ideas about psychology and epistemology into his book entitled *The Philosophy of Rhetoric*.

It was no coincidence that a twentieth-century British semanticist and literary critic, I. A. Richards, also called his 1936 work *The Philosophy of Rhetoric*. Unlike Campbell, however, Richards rejected the whole flow of classical rhetorical thought—"sales talk selling sales talk," he called it—and argued for a rhetoric that would entail "a study of misunderstanding and its remedies," a scientific approach to the study of language at its elemental levels (Richards 3). The idea of training persuaders was abhorrent to Richards, who believed that modern readers needed to be able to arm themselves *against* skillful persuaders. Richards' "philosophy of rhetoric" thus rested upon a metaphysical groundwork that would have been entirely alien to George Campbell.

As we saw in Chapter 1, the theory of argumentation espoused by Chaim Perelman, which he called *la nouvelle rhétorique*, resulted from his philosophic mission: to find a rational basis for decision making in the fields of human endeavor where the doctrines of Cartesian rationalism, the canons of formal logic, and the procedures of modern mathematics have proven to be ineffectual. Perelman was, first and foremost, a *philosopher*. His writings stress the interrelationships between rhetoric and philosophy at every turn, and anyone who essays to understand his rhetorical views must first examine the metaphysical axioms upon which they are based. Unlike Campbell or Richards, whose titles promised a more spacious treatment of their subjects than their books fulfilled, Perelman's theory embraces a coherent world view in which rhetoric plays an essential part. In this chapter, we will scrutinize the philosophical assumptions underlying the New Rhetoric.

The governing idea of this chapter is that Perelman's opposition to classical rationalism, which sought unique truth and certitude about its conclusions, led him to enlarge the domain of reason to encompass a rhetorical rationalism that allows for a pluralism of values and a multiplicity of ways of being reasonable. Our adumbration of this thesis will lead us to examine four aspects of Perelman's thought: (1) his conception of the philosophical enterprise itself; (2) the theory of knowledge upon which his rhetorical views are based; (3) the jurisprudential "logic" that resulted from his analysis of justice; and (4) the concept of rhetorical reason, the culmination of his philosophic efforts.

Perelman's Conception of Philosophy

From the outset of his career as an undergraduate scholar at the Free University of Brussels until his death, Perelman strove assiduously to establish the philosophical method as a necessary mode of viewing human beings and their problems. For him, philosophy played a role in the clarification of the human condition that science could never usurp. As we noted in Chapter 1, at one time in his career he perceived a similarity between the deductive logical structures of philosophy and science. That analogy did not extend far, however, and his postwar writings manifest an abiding skepticism concerning the capacity of science to deal with the most pressing of human enigmas. In a critique of Auguste Comte's positivism, he wrote:

> It cannot be denied that Comte's analysis is correct regarding certain areas of knowledge where scientific answers have completely replaced theological or philosophical concepts. But that is quite another thing from saying that *all* human problems can be solved by calling on the experimental or deductive methods of science alone. The study not of what is but of what ought to be,

> what has the greater value, what is preferable, and what should determine our choices and our conduct can be abandoned to scientific methods only when we are dealing with purely technical problems. But that is far from being the case. Not only does the solution of our fundamental problems elude science and technology; the very hypothesis that philosophy can be dispensed with is itself a philosophical hypothesis. (*Historical Introduction* 5–6)

Although Perelman believed in the indispensability of philosophy, his conception of its mission differed from the views of earlier philosophers who attempted to base their systems on necessary or self-evident theses. Whereas traditional metaphysics had always tried to uncover eternal and immutable principles, Perelman believed that philosophy should "elaborate principles of being, thought, and action that are humanly *reasonable*" ("On Self-Evidence" 5–6). The interminable controversies that marked the whole history of philosophic thought were due, as he saw it, not to obscurity or to the positive errors of philosophers, but to the nature of the enterprise itself. In philosophy, the methods of formal logic are practically useless: "The goal of philosophy is to influence the mind and win its agreement, rather than to perform purely formal transformations of propositions" (*Historical Introduction* 101).

In Perelman's view, the contingent nature of the axioms of every metaphysical system necessitates a recourse to rhetoric. Even the rationalists, who try to eliminate every value conflict from their vision of the universe, "arrive at their ends only after having imposed, thanks to rhetoric, their fundamental principles," and, so long as the superiority of their system is not admitted, they must "resort to the processes of rhetorical argumentation" ("Réflexions" 280–281). Besides using rhetoric to promote a world view, philosophers employ it to make ethical judgments. In his 1967 book, *Justice*, Perelman said:

> The specific role of philosophy is, in effect, to propose to humanity objective principles of action that will be valid for the will of all reasonable men. This objectivity will not consist either in conformity to some exterior object or in submission to the commands of any particular authority. It envisages an ideal of universality and constitutes an attempt to formulate norms and values such as could be proposed to every reasonable being. (78)

We will consider the "ideal of universality" and the notion of "all reasonable men" later in this chapter, and in conjunction with our discussion of Perelman's notion of audience in Chapter 3. For now, it is sufficient to note that in proposing ethical values, as in elaborating a world view, every philosopher falls back upon axioms whose fallibility excludes them from either the realm of scientific demonstration or from the domain of formal logic.

Even if the principles of a philosophical system were granted by everyone, there is no reason to suppose its conclusions would be universally accepted. Because proof in philosophy is not simply a transposition in the order of postulations and theorems as in the deductive sciences of mathematics or geometry, the "conclusions are quite different from the original premises, and the process of arriving at them can only be explained by a difference in the nature of the proof." Hence, Spinoza's ideal of a geometric, deductive, rationalistic philosophy can never be attained. In Perelman's view, "A philosophical system cannot be proved like a treatise in geometry" (*Historical Introduction* 101, 140).

Perelman's own conception of the nature of philosophy is revealed most clearly in a distinction he made between two types of philosophy: primary philosophies and regressive philosophy. Most traditional systems have been of the former type. They have tried to construct an edifice of universal, immutable truths. No provision has been made for future modifications. Consequently, when a crack appears in its foundation, the "primary" philosopher has been forced to admit a mistake, to attribute his or her error to spurious evidence or to a fallacious view of necessity, and then, after making the necessary changes, to rebuild the structure as solidly as possible, and to proceed again to defend it to the last assault. Regressive philosophy, on the other hand, affirms that every philosopher starts with facts that are neither necessary, nor absolute, nor definitive, but which are sufficient to permit the grounding of his or her thought. Unlike primary philosophy, "every crisis in its foundations constitutes, for regressive philosophy, a confirmation, a deepening of thought, for which it can only rejoice" ("Philosophies Premières" 190). When compelled to modify a system of thought, the philosopher simply chooses from among alternative possibilities the one deemed to be best. Of course, the choice must then be justified; reasons have to be presented, if agreement is to be obtained from the community of philosophical peers (184–185). Perelman's preference for regressive philosophy can be explained succinctly: Philosophizing is a *human* endeavor whose function cannot be replaced by science; its methods are rhetorical and argumentative, rather than deductive and mathematical; and philosophers should entertain no delusion that their premises and conclusions are necessary or irrefragable. Not surprisingly, this regressive philosophy engenders a distinctive epistemology.

Perelman's Theory of Knowledge

The idea that what passes for knowledge is always a sociological construction based upon agreements among groups in a certain milieu came early to Chaim Perelman, while he was still a student at the University of Brussels. Following his master Dupréel's affirmation that human communities coalesce around shared values, the 21-year old doctoral candidate advanced the thesis that an arbitrary element lies at the base of every "necessary" truth ("De l'Arbitraire" 35). "The problems of the theory of knowledge, like those of morality," he maintained, "seem to us to resolve themselves most easily through the consideration of rapports among multiple groups" (41). These agreements, or "adherences" as he would later come to call them, are necessary from the start of collaboration, since members of a particular community—historians, jurists, philosophers, scientists, and so forth—have to decide upon the rules and means of verification they will accept as touchstones for according the status of knowledge to particular ideas in their respective domains.

In a sense, Perelman's philosophic quest for a logic of value judgments was a search for a rational basis for adjudicating truth claims among disputed and conflicting notions. By the end of the 1940s, after he and his co-worker Olbrechts-Tyteca had "rediscovered" the argumentative techniques used in antiquity for establishing agreements, the epistemological ramifications of their findings were becoming evident. In 1950 the Belgians published a lengthy essay, "Logique et Rhétorique," in which they concluded:

> We believe that a theory of knowledge which corresponds to this climate of contemporary philosophy needs to integrate into its structure the processes of argumentation utilized in every domain of human culture and that . . . a renewal of rhetoric would conform to the humanist aspect of the aspirations of our age. (35)

Before we examine Perelman's view of knowledge in detail, it is helpful to consider his critique of the shortcomings found in earlier theories.

After surveying the epistemologies set forth by the rationalists, empiricists, and logical positivists, Perelman concluded that these philosophies all failed to grasp one fundamental fact: While it is possible to quantify physical phenomena, the same cannot be said for mental phenomena. In his *Critique of Pure Reason*, Immanuel Kant had recognized that intensive magnitude is of a wholly different order from extensive magnitude. This insight paved the way for Henri Bergson's analysis: "Bergson showed that psychological phenomena are qualitatively different from each other and that we cannot apply calculation or measure to them" (*Historical Introduction* 186). Another weakness in the earlier model of an eternal and unchanging reason was its inability to account for historical and social conditions. Any viable theory of knowledge must include such factors, and this realization caused Perelman to assign to rhetoric a primary role in the shaping of knowledge. For him, rhetoric, which had been entirely ignored by Descartes and his followers, serves an indispensable methodological role in the sociology of knowledge. In a 1950 article, he presented his rationale for studying rhetoric:

> To determine the field of application of the sociology of knowledge, it would be necessary to study most closely this strange logic [rhetoric] and the reasons which make it undergo the influence of social and cultural factors. One would see upon analysis that the proofs which govern it are neither the evidence of calculus nor experimental evidence, but those which Aristotle called "dialectical proofs," and which he studied in his *Topics* and his *Rhetoric*. . . . Only a detailed examination of rhetorical argumentation will permit the founding of the sociology of knowledge upon the most solid bases. ("Sociologie de la Connaissance" 315).

As Perelman realized, a study of the argumentative devices used to describe and explain phenomena introduces the element of language into any modern theory of knowledge. Classical rationalists had failed to grasp the problems associated with the communication of meaning through linguistic symbols. The doctrine that self-evidence founded on the identity of subject and object can lay claim to the truth was based upon a fundamental misconception: "Every assertion, before it can be judged true or false, must first be meaningful. Linguistic statements are made up of symbols which, by definition, cannot coincide with what they designate" ("On Self-Evidence" 13). Perelman reasoned that it was not possible to identify the truth of a judgment with the self-evidence of an intuition. The best rationalists could do was to "make the intervention of language as inoffensive as possible in order to render perfectly transparent the veil it cannot help but be" (16–17). Perelman rejected the extreme positions taken by both the "realists" and the "nominalists":

> The choice of a linguistic form is neither purely arbitrary nor simply a carbon copy of reality. The reasons that induce us to prefer one conception of experience, one analogy, to another, are a function of our vision of the world. The form is not separable from the content; language is not a veil which one need only discard or render transparent in order to perceive the

> real as such; it is inextricably bound up with a point of view, with the taking of a position. ("Rhetoric and Philosophy" 16–17)

Language is a human artifact, Perelman believed, but "it is not produced by an irrational decision of a single individual. It develops, normally, in the midst of a community, the members of which can modify it by the use they make of it as soon as they consider there are any reasons for promoting any change" (*Idea of Justice* 123).

The deficiencies in earlier epistemologies appeared to be most pronounced in classical rationalism, and Perelman's work is, in large part, devoted to the overthrow of the Cartesian theory of knowledge. The view stemming from Descartes that science is a collection of facts that have been established and definitively remain so is, to Perelman's way of thinking, "a theory of knowledge which is not human, but divine; of knowledge acquired by a unique and perfect Being, without initiation, training, tradition or need to learn. On this view, the history of knowledge, on its positive side, becomes uniquely that of additions, not that of successive modifications" (*Idea of Justice* 116–117). Such a notion is, of course, antithetical to Perelman's "regressive" philosophy. Rather than placing emphasis on the *results* obtained by the scientific method, the advocate of the "new rhetoric" stressed the *process* by which scientific theories become accepted:

> If we assume that the sciences develop on the basis of opinions previously accepted—and replaced by others either when difficulty results from some contradiction or in order to allow of new elements of knowledge being integrated in the theory—then the understanding of scientific methodology requires us to be concerned not with building the scientific edifice on the foundation of self-evident truths, but with indicating why and how certain accepted opinions come to be no longer regarded as the most probable and the most suitable to express our beliefs, and are replaced by others. The history of the evolution of scientific ideas would be highly revealing in this regard. (*Idea of Justice* 94)

From Perelman's perspective, "neither the self-evident principles of the rationalists nor the irrefragable facts of the empiricists constitute clear and distinct elements of knowledge which no subsequent progress could later modify or make more specific" (95). Not only have the rationalistic and empiricist ideas "generated misconceptions about the role of language and the methodology of the sciences," as H. L. A. Hart observes in the Introduction to Perelman's book, *The Idea of Justice and the Problem of Argument*, but by conceiving knowledge as "a structure at the base of which is an indubitable experience of sense-given data," they have led to an altogether "misleading contrast between knowledge and opinion" (xi). As we will see later in this chapter, Perelman attempted to remove this unnecessary distinction by promulgating an enlarged concept of reason.

Perelman's view of knowledge paralleled, and in some respects was influenced by, the work of theoretical physicists and philosophers of science whose ideas had challenged the positivistic assumptions inherited from the nineteenth century. The notion of science as a body of timeless and objective truths had been shaken by the theories of relativity, quantum mechanics, and Werner Heisenberg's relations of indeterminacy. Perelman's own investigations into the paradoxes of logic in the 1930s had underscored for him the uncertainty the scholarly world was beginning to feel about the rationality inherent in the received view of the universe. Efforts to shore up the traditional dogma had failed. In a 1970 essay on "Scientific Methodology and Open Philosophy," Perelman discussed the paradigmatic shift that was occurring:

> It took some time for the scientific revolution to find an adequate expression in the theory of knowledge. Henri Poincaré's conventionalism, Hilbert's formalism and the Platonizing intuitionism of a Frege and a Husserl, could not provide a theory adequate to the scientific demand because none of them took into account the way the sciences evolved and progressed, integrating into a new formulation what should be preserved from old results. It is only since the second half of this century that a richer and more complete vision of scientific activity began to dominate our culture, placing at the center of our preoccupations not the results of the scientific procedure formulated in the form of propositions but this procedure itself in the concreteness of its evolution, taking into account, much more than previously, its social and historical dimensions. (*New Rhetoric and the Humanities* 101)

As evidence of the stress that was now being placed on the cultural and social aspects of an individual scholar's role in the scientific community, Perelman pointed to such works as Thomas S. Kuhn's *The Structure of Scientific Revolutions* and Michael Polanyi's *Personal Knowledge*. In particular, Polanyi has demonstrated that the individual scientist's talent and skill intervenes at every step of the scientific process, from the elaboration of hypotheses through the verification of experimental results. The "knowledge" thus obtained depends upon the flair and intuition of the scientist, as well as upon the established tradition of which the scientist is a part. By stressing the creative aspect of scientific activity, Polanyi reveals the close connections between the personal decisions made by a scientist and other forms of culture, such as art and religion. Indeed the passionate commitment of the scientist to his or her intellectual mission is quite analogous to the feelings aroused in one who struggles for a noble cause or is devoted to a cult of beauty.

Intrigued by Polanyi's ideas, Perelman believed them to add substantially to a critique of the foundations of contemporary positivism. In one important respect, however, Perelman parted company with Polanyi's theory of science:

> To my mind, [Polanyi] likens the personal involvement of the scientist too much to that of the artist or the philosopher. I believe there are essential differences. Even if, like Polanyi, I am a partisan of personal knowledge integrated with a cultural tradition, I should still like to stress the particular place of science in our culture. For, in science, the techniques of proof and verification make it possible to bring about agreement in essentials, an accord inaccessible in other domains. ("Polanyi's Interpretation" 241)

The spirit of Polanyi's assault on positivism found a sympathetic echo in the Belgian philosopher's regressive philosophy, but the latter's epistemology had a distinctly rhetorical cast: scientific knowledge, as Perelman conceived it, was nothing but the agreements reached by the community of scientists who adhered to particular methods of investigation and means of verifying the results of their studies.

Perelman's views about knowledge had shifted considerably by the mid-1940s. His 1933 essay, "De l'Arbitraire dans la Connaissance," had reflected the rationalistic assumptions of his intellectual community. One reviewer of this essay detected a resemblance between Perelman's notions about the arbitrariness inherent in the postulates on which knowledge is built and the contemporaneous ideas of the American philosopher, C. I. Lewis (Costello 613). Although there is no evidence of a direct linkage, both Perelman and Lewis underwent a similar metamorphosis in their thinking about the status of knowledge claims. In his 1946 book, *An Analysis of Knowledge and Valuation*, Lewis reached a conclusion nearly identical to the results Perelman obtained from his meticulous analysis of the concept of justice. Wrote Lewis:

> Knowledge is not a descriptive but a normative category: it claims correctness; mental states are classified as genuine knowing only on assumption of such correctness. Epistemology is not psychological description of such mental states, but is critique of their cognitive claim; the assessment of their veracity and validity, and the eliciting of those criteria by which such claim may be attested. (Lewis 10–11)

Like Lewis, who was concerned with the criteria by which cognitive claims can be judged, Perelman stressed the importance of justifying one's fundamental postulates:

> For centuries logicians have been able to neglect the problem of the justification of one's choice of axioms, by considering the latter either as self-evident or as arbitrary. In the first case, since we must bow to the evidence, we have no choice and therefore no need to justify our acceptance. In the second case, since all choices are considered equally arbitrary, it is impossible to justify any one by showing it to be preferable to any other. When we reject both of these extremes, so reminiscent of realism and nominalism, when we admit that a choice of axioms is possible and that it is not entirely arbitrary, then the justification of choice ceases to be a negligible problem. (*Justice* 60)

The rejection of both self-evidence and its extreme opposite, arbitrariness, had the effect of blurring the distinction between knowledge and opinion that had been the basis of Cartesian epistemology. Perelman was willing to accord "the status of knowledge to a tested opinion, to an opinion, that is, which has survived all objections and criticisms and with regard to which we have a certain confidence, though no certainty, that it will resist all such future attacks" (*Idea of Justice* 117). Unlike Lewis, Polanyi, and other critics of rationalism, Perelman posited a theory of knowledge that emphasizes the *reasons* we have for deciding in a particular way as well as the *techniques of reasoning* by which we arrive at those decisions. In his view, an epistemology should be "founded on what a theory of the nature of argumentation, as it actually is, can teach us" (122). Given this premise, it was natural for a philosopher trained in law to turn to jurisprudence for assistance in finding out how arguments actually work in a setting of disputed claims.

The Judicial Model of Reasoning

When Chaim Perelman undertook his analysis of justice while the Germans still occupied Belgium, he did not expect to open up the entire process of rhetorical justification for scrutiny. His goals were much more modest. "I was still imbued with positivist philosophy," he confessed four decades later. "I believed that the only acceptable method for studying the idea was to clarify it by emptying it of its emotive aspect which shows itself every time one discusses the notion of justice, because this notion designates a universal value which everyone respects but which everyone conceives in his own way"

(*Justice, Law, and Argument* 99). However, Perelman's "positivistic" analysis was not conducted in a philosophical vacuum; he could trace efforts to locate a core meaning for justice at least back to Aristotle. Extraordinary confusion, he found, had surrounded the idea of justice throughout history; it appeared as the supreme rational virtue in Greek philosophy, as an impassioned invocation in Jewish prophecy, and as a rather technical legal concept in Roman jurisprudence.

How was Perelman to make sense of all these multifarious meanings? He decided to take an inventory of the denotations of the word "justice" and found six different meanings currently in use:

1. To each the same thing.
2. To each according to his merits.
3. To each according to his works.
4. To each according to his needs.
5. To each according to his rank.
6. To each according to his legal entitlement (*Idea of Justice* 7).

Faced with these disparate conceptions of justice, Perelman looked for an underlying commonality independent of semantic connotations or ideological implications (Stone, *Human Law* 302). The answer appeared in the form of a formal, abstract principle, similar to the notion of intrinsic equality, which Perelman codified as *formal justice: "a principle of action in accordance with which beings of one and the same essential category must be treated in the same way"* (*Idea of Justice* 16). This definition did not address the question of what "essential categories" should count in the administration of justice. Although it satisfied Perelman's philosophical leanings at that point in his career, the principle of "formal justice" had obvious shortcomings as a formula for concrete justice. Clearly the determination of what constitutes "essentially similar cases" and how they are to be applied in actual practice renders value judgments inescapable. Neither experience nor calculation can serve as a basis for such an application; the equality at the root of the idea of justice was exposed as a purely formal affair, and the foundations of Perelman's positivism began to shake. The decision to select a specific criterion (needs, rank, legal entitlement, etc.) for evaluating justice seemed to be arbitrary. To attempt a universal validation of any such norm would lead to an infinite regress, since the standard upon which that norm was based would have to be justified, and so on. Such reasoning led Perelman to conclude that there could be no perfect justice.

Even though an arbitrary element always crowds its way into any normative system, thus flouting formal justice, the general principle Perelman had uncovered proved to be useful beyond the realm of ethics or moral behavior. Indeed it promised to elucidate the problem of justification in its broadest extent. "Justification," Perelman came to believe, "can deal with legality, morality, regularity (in the widest sense of the word), usefulness or expediency" ("Value Judgments" 46). Furthermore, the idea of justification implies the "possibility of an unfavorable appraisal of what you are trying to justify" (46). Under such conditions, rational arguments are called forth, and the abstract principle of Perelman's is transformed into a *rule of justice* that can be used to determine the relative strength of arguments:

> It is useless to try to define rational argumentation the way we define a demonstrative technique, namely, by its conformity to certain prescribed rules. Unlike demonstrative reasoning, arguments are never correct or incorrect; they are either strong or weak, relevant or irrelevant. The strength or weakness is judged according to the Rule of Justice, which requires that essentially similar situations be treated in the same manner. (*Justice* 83)

Relevance or irrelevance, Perelman goes on to say, is a matter to be determined by the rules and criteria recognized by the appropriate disciplines and their methodologies. But the salient point here is that Perelman's analysis of justice provided a yardstick for assessing the strength of arguments that, by their very nature, cannot be judged according to the rules of formal logic.

The insight that the "rule of justice" could be applied to *any problem of justification* was a crucial development in the system of thought that became the New Rhetoric. As a formalistic element, however, it lacked any practical significance in concrete legal settings, for it failed to surmount the arbitrariness inherent in the selection and application of values in a specific judicial proceeding. Legal theorist H. L. A. Hart recognized the limitations of such a rule:

> We must know when, for the purposes in hand, cases are to be regarded as alike and what differences are relevant. Without this further supplement we cannot proceed to criticize laws or other social arrangements as unjust. It is not unjust for the law when it forbids homicide to treat red-haired murderers in the same way as others; indeed it would be unjust if it treated them differently, as it would be if it refused to treat differently the sane and the insane. (Hart 155)

Perelman also saw these deficiencies. "If the Rule of Justice is not always adequate for a just application of the law," he said, "it is altogether powerless when it comes to judging the law itself—that is, to determining whether the law is just or unjust. In effect, the Rule of Justice tells us nothing about the content of rules" (*Justice, Law, and Argument* 41).

Given the fact that neither formal justice nor its normative offspring can guarantee tangible justice, how are we ever going to attain any decision worthy of the honorific connotations traditionally associated with the term "justice"? For Perelman, when values clash or simultaneous account must be taken of a plurality of "essential characteristics" (both "rank" and "need," for example), another concept, *equity*, must come to the rescue. Equity can be regarded as "the crutch of justice," an indispensable complement to formal justice. Aristotle foreshadowed this notion in the *Ethics* when he said that "the equitable is just, but not the legally just but a correction of legal justice," and in the *Rhetoric*, where he called equity "the sort of justice which goes beyond the written law" (*Ethica Nicomachea* 1137b 11–14; *Rhetoric* 1374a 27). Although Perelman had probably not yet encountered the *Rhetoric* when he formulated his ideas on justice, he was certainly familiar with Aristotle's ethical writings. Of greater influence on him than classical sources, however, was his own education in jurisprudence.

It seemed obvious to Perelman that a "logic" was at work in the courtroom, one that differed considerably from the formal or mathematical kind practiced by contemporary logicians. In his preface to Georges Kalinowski's *Introduction à la Logique Juridique*, Perelman wrote:

> When the jurist defends a *logical* interpretation of law, when his [or her] opponents retort that "the life of law is not *logic*, but experience," when advocates accuse each other of not respecting *logic*, the word "logic" does not designate in any of these cases formal logic, the only one practiced by the majority of professional logicians, but juridical logic, which modern logicians entirely ignore. (v)

Under most western legal systems, the judge is *required*—even in the absence of compelling evidence—to interpret the law, to justify its application to the immediate case, and to render a decision in accordance with the provisions of the law. According to Perelman, "juridical logic" functions as the intellectual instrument enabling the judge to fulfill these obligations.

As he pursued his quest for a logic of value judgments in conjunction with Olbrechts-Tyteca during the 1950s, Perelman came to realize that judicial logic is similar to the process of deliberating about values outside the courtroom. "Ratiocination about values," he decided, "is much more like a juridical argument than a mathematical deduction" ("How Do We Apply

Reason to Values?" 798). Meanwhile, the English logician Stephen Toulmin had reached a similar conclusion, albeit from a different philosophical perspective. In *The Uses of Argument*, published in 1958 when the French edition of *The New Rhetoric* also appeared, Toulmin said: "Logic (we may say) is generalised jurisprudence. Arguments can be compared with lawsuits, and the claims we make and argue for in extra-legal contexts with claims made in the courts, while the cases we present in making good each kind of claim can be compared with each other" (Toulmin 7). Toulmin's search for a "working logic" applicable to human decision-making paralleled the Belgian's research agenda, although he did not undertake a formalistic analysis of justice or link his work to classical rhetoric and dialectic. Both Toulmin and Perelman turned to a judicial model of reasoning, however, "as an aid for their philosophical tasks" (Stone, *Legal System* 335). In their hands juridical reasoning came to be used as a paradigm for the entire field of nonformal logic.

One axiom of the judicial model illustrates its applicability to all instances in which justifications are called forth: the rationality of treating essentially similar beings alike. The rule of justice posits a continuity of thought and action that assigns preference to the normal, the recurring, and the customary. Perelman followed the doctrine espoused by Quintilian, Whately, and others that presumption favors the *status quo:* "Law teaches us to abandon existing rules only if good reasons justify their replacement: Only change requires justification, presumption playing in favor of what exists, just as the burden of proof falls upon him who wants to change an established state of affairs" (*Justice* 104). The reliance upon precedents in legal reasoning rests upon this doctrine of presumption, which is itself a manifestation of the law of *inertia.* Influenced by Schopenhauer, who considered inertia a law of the will, Perelman saw it as controlling human beliefs and behaviors just as it does the motions of physical objects. He explained the psychological basis of inertia in this way:

> The fact is, the rule of justice results from a tendency, natural to the human mind to regard as normal and rational, and so requiring no supplementary justification, a course of behaviour in conformity with precedent. In any social order, then, everything that is traditional will appear to be a matter of course. *Per contra* every deviation, every change, will have to be justified. This situation, which results from the application of the principle of inertia in the life of the mind, explains the role played by tradition. It is tradition that is taken as a starting-point, it is tradition that is criticised and it is tradition that is maintained in so far as no reason is seen for departing from it.

> And this holds good in the most diverse fields—ethics or law, science or philosophy. (*Idea of Justice* 86)

Viewed from Perelman's lofty philosophical perspective, inertia is "the basis of the stability of our spiritual and social life" (*New Rhetoric and the Humanities* 131). It becomes an encompassing explanatory principle in *The New Rhetoric*, where it is operationalized in the form of presumptions, which serve as bases or starting points of argument.

In brief review, we see that Perelman's analysis of justice revealed a principle of action, formalized as the rule of justice, which pervades all rational activity. His search for a logic of value judgments led him (and Olbrechts-Tyteca) to "rediscover" the dialectical and rhetorical proofs of Aristotle. Both strands of his research then conjoined to produce an expansive view of reason.

The Concept of Rhetorical Reason

By the time *The New Rhetoric* was published, it was clear that Perelman had an expansive and ambitious philosophical goal in mind. He hoped to establish a rational basis for human decision making. His own intellectual odyssey was complete; he had shed the positivistic assumptions of his early career. Yet the influence of two groups—the Cartesian rationalists and the modern mathematical logicians—was still paramount in the philosophical community of which he was part. These groups shared the responsibility, he believed, for the constricted view of reason that still prevailed:

> The logician, inspired by the Cartesian ideal, feels at home only in the study of the proofs that Aristotle qualified as analytic. No other means presents the same character of necessity. And this tendency is all the more strongly marked after a period in which, under the influence of the mathematical logicians, logic was reduced to formal logic, to a study of the means of proof used in the mathematical sciences. As a result, reasoning which is foreign to the purely formal domain escapes logic, and consequently escapes reason too. ("The New Rhetoric" 5)

Perelman believed that the narrowing of the field of logic to the study of formal reasoning had disastrous effects on the human sciences, on law and on all branches of philosophy.

To understand Perelman's philosophical stance, it is necessary to distinguish between two types of reason—the logical and the rhetorical. A logical system consists of a set of propositions and rules removed from time. Its data are isolated from every context except itself; its instruments are fixed. These instruments are correct expressions and rules of inference. Rhetoric, by contrast, explores the domain of concrete and situated reason. It functions as a tool of rationality within the expanded scope of a "regressive" philosophy. In his review essay, "Rhetoric as the Logic of the Behavioral Sciences," Max Loreau explained the notion of rhetorical reason:

> Its investigation bears upon discourse which allows a place to the non-conventional, to the implicit, to the indeterminate; it aspires to the explication and to the structuration of the systems of reasoning used implicitly in the discursive exploitation of the margin of indetermination which affects ideas and which is manifested when the meaning attributed to these latter finds itself contested either by a new truth or by a new situation. (Loreau 457–458)

Rhetorical reason does not merely discover truth and error; it also justifies and argues. It broadens the idea of what is reasonable well beyond the analytical, the demonstrative, and the calculable.

When the full reverberations of Perelman's expanded definition of reason are felt, the traditional separation of the will from the understanding, reminiscent of faculty psychology, disappears, carrying with it the conviction-persuasion dichotomy that has plagued rhetorical theory for centuries. Perelman thought this dualism could be traced back to Aristotle, who devoted his *Topics* to the theoretical discussion of theses and his *Rhetoric* to the peculiarities of audiences. Whatever its origins, the division between convincing and persuading was based upon a faulty psychological premise. Human beings are not made up of distinctly separate faculties and "the conviction-persuasion opposition cannot suffice when one leaves the bounds of a strict rationalism and examines the diverse means of obtaining the adherence of minds" ("Logique et Rhétorique" 7).

By extending the domain of reason, Perelman hoped to give a rational basis to law, ethics, philosophy, political debate, and other fields in which logic in the strict sense could not be considered relevant. When he and Olbrechts-Tyteca began to examine the processes of actual argument, they sought out "arguments put forward by advertisers in newspapers, politicians in speeches, lawyers in pleadings, judges in decisions, and philosophers in treatises" (*The New Rhetoric* 10). A truly practical logic, they believed, must apply to all of these areas.

Summary

The philosophical substructure of Perelman's theory of rhetoric has been laid out clearly in his hundreds of writings, beginning with the earliest essays he wrote as a student at the University of Brussels. His rejection of the rationalist doctrines of self-evidence and the uniqueness of truth, which had occurred by the mid-1940s, led him to conceive the aim of philosophy to be the setting forth and *justification* of a defensible world view. Since one's fundamental axioms are neither self-evident nor necessary, he reasoned that only rational argumentation can supply such justification.

As we have seen, the presuppositions inherent in Perelman's "regressive" philosophy emphasize the role of decision in the acquisition and transmission of knowledge. The positivistic notion that our knowledge constitutes an edifice of immutable truths is shattered by the realization that the truth of our beliefs cannot be guaranteed once and for all. As Perelman maintained, such truths "are worked out, made specific and refined—and these truths constitute no more than the best tested of our opinions" (*Idea of Justice* 133). The principal result of this revelation was to remove the dubious distinction between knowledge and opinion.

In search of a principle of justification that can rightly claim to be rational, Perelman found in his analysis of justice a common, abstract element at the base of the various conceptions of justice: the idea that beings of the same essential category must be treated alike. The arbitrariness inherent in deciding upon the "essential categories" renders absolute justice impossible and highlights the need for a logic of value judgments. Perelman's earnest and systematic hunt for such a logic, carried out in the company of his devoted co-worker, Lucie Olbrechts-Tyteca, led to an unexpected fountainhead—the argumentative techniques Aristotle had classified as dialectical and rhetorical proofs.

In the European intellectual community of the 1950s, the idea that a Belgian professor of law, logic, and metaphysics would seriously propose the development of a general theory of argumentation inspired by classical rhetoric seemed preposterous. But his indictment of the restrictive and impractical view of rationality passed down from Descartes, Pascal, and their successors was potent, if not irrefutable. Operating in the realm of the probable, the contingent, and the plausible, Perelman's enlarged concept of reason was needed to place law, philosophy, and the behavioral sciences on a rational footing.

The philosophical postulates we have examined in this chapter are foundational to an adequate understanding of Perelman's rhetorical enterprise. So is another concept, the idea of audience. Indeed the theory of argumentation developed by the Belgians might well have been called the New Dialectic, had it not been for two considerations: first, the term dialectic had undergone a confusing metamorphosis since the time of Aristotle, especially at the hands of Hegel and Marx; and, second, the ancient theories of rhetoric all placed the concept of audience at their center. For these reasons, and in light of his ambitious intellectual agenda, Perelman enunciated the most expansive and philosophically nuanced conception of the rhetorical audience found in any of the "new rhetorics" of the twentieth century.

CHAPTER 3

A Theory of the Rhetorical Audience

Like all rhetorical theorists, from Gorgias on, Perelman and Olbrechts-Tyteca believe that audience is at the very center of matters rhetorical "since argumentation aims at securing the adherence of those to whom it is addressed, it is, in its entirety, relative to the audience to be influenced" (19). But Perelman and Olbrechts-Tyteca differ from their predecessors in that they have a complete theory, a coherent idea of what a rhetorical audience is. This truth about their work has been obscured by a lengthy debate concerning the value of one part of that theory, their concept of the universal audience. It has not been clearly understood that this concept cannot be comprehended if it is isolated from the theory as a whole. In this chapter, we will discuss this theory. We will show that, for Perelman and Olbrechts-Tyteca, all rhetorical audiences, both universal and particular, are constructed, the difference being that in the case of the former, speakers aim at transformation or reinforcement in the areas of fact, truth, and presumption, while in the latter, they aim at transformation or reinforcement in the area of values.

What do these categories mean? Together, fact, truth, and presumption constitute what we regard as real. It is a fact that the earth is a planet; it is a truth of Newtonian physics that every action has an equal and opposite reaction; it is a presumption that the quality of an act reveals the quality of the person. Values embody the preferable, the guidelines for the way we judge ourselves and others. If we are French, for example, we may prefer the abstract values of liberty, equality, and fraternity, as well as the concrete values of things quintessentially French: French cuisine, French philosophy and literature, France itself. Philosophy and science are the paradigm examples of discourses in which facts, truths, and presumptions are central;

these are discourses that aim at a universal audience, the imagined community of all rational beings. On the other hand, public address is the paradigm example of discourse focused primarily at values, on the preferable, discourse aimed at an imagined community of particular beings: Americans, the Elks, the elderly.

Any discussion of Perelman and Olbrechts-Tyteca's view of the rhetorical audience must acknowledge the deeply contested debate concerning the most original of their concepts, the universal audience. John Ray, Henry Johnstone, and Lisa Ede have all mounted arguments against the coherence, and the usefulness of this idea. Ede must stand for the rest when she says that Perelman and Olbrechts-Tyteca are caught in a trap of their own making, a contradiction between their fundamental belief that any plausible theory of argumentation must assail the idea of self-evidence, and their assertion that "argumentation addressed to the universal audience must convince the reader that the reasons adduced are of a compelling character, that they are self evident, and possess an absolute timeless validity, independent of local or historical contingencies" (32). Indeed, Perelman himself pays tribute to the cogency of such criticisms when he says that "it is the notion of the universal audience which has created the most misunderstandings among my rhetorical readers" (*The New Rhetoric*, 190). It is our view, however, that Perelman and Olbrechts-Tyteca use the concept of universal audience consistently, and that it is part of a theoretically coherent concept of audience with considerable potential as a tool for rhetorical criticism.

Perelman and Olbrechts-Tyteca believe that all rhetorical audiences are constructed by the speaker. Of course there are real audiences; of course their study poses a genuine problem; but it is a challenge, they feel, beyond the scope of rhetoric: the study of real audiences is the business of experimental psychology. "We shall proceed differently. We seek . . . to characterize the different argumentative structures, the analysis of which must precede all experimental tests of their effectiveness" (9). From this we may infer Perelman and Olbrechts-Tyteca's central tenet that all rhetorical audiences must be constructed by the speaker: "The audience, as visualized by one undertaking to argue, is always a more or less systematized construction" (19). Moreover, this rhetorical audience is always composite: Since real audiences must consist of disparate individuals with differing convictions of differing intensity, and since no algorithm exists that can combine these differences conceptually, the achievement of a synthetic unity must be a consequence of the speaker's intuition. In their opening remarks—indeed throughout their speeches—speakers must embody their best guesses of their audiences' views of the two components of this systematical unity, the twin categories of the real and the preferable:

> An orator does not have to be confronted with several organized factions to think of the composite nature of his audience. He is justified in visualizing each one of his listeners as simultaneously belonging to a number of disparate groups. Even when an orator stands before only a few auditors, or indeed, before a single auditor, it is possible that he will not be quite sure what arguments will appear most convincing to his audience. In such a case, he will, by a kind of fiction, insert his audience into a series of different audiences. (22)

Perelman and Olbrechts-Tyteca's example is from the novel, *Tristram Shandy*, in which Tristram's father persuades his wife to have a midwife by arguing "like a Christian, like a heathen, like a husband, like a father, like a patriot, like a man" (22).

If all audiences are constructed, then their views of the real and the preferable, as imagined by the speaker, must form the initial common ground between speaker and audience, the starting points of any argumentation. To illustrate the real, we will use the exordium of the "Cooper Institute" Address of February 27, 1860, a beginning in which Abraham Lincoln rehearses the components of the real, the matters of fact and of truth that he believes he shares with his audience:

> Mr. President and fellow citizens of New York:—
>
> The facts with which I shall deal this evening are mainly old and familiar; nor is there anything new in the general use I shall make of them. If there shall be any novelty, it will be in the mode of presenting the facts, and the inferences and observations following that presentation.
>
> In his speech last autumn, at Columbus, Ohio, as reported in "The New York Times," Senator Douglas said:
>
> "*Our fathers, when they framed the Government under which we live, understood this question just as well, and even better than we do now.*"
>
> I fully indorse this, and I adopt it as a text for this discourse. I so adopt it because it furnishes a precise and an agreed starting point for a discussion between Republicans and that wing of the Democracy headed by Senator Douglas. It simply leaves the inquiry: "*What was the understanding those fathers had of the question mentioned?*"
>
> What is the frame of government under which we live?
>
> The answer must be: "The Constitution of the United States." That Constitution consists of the original, framed in 1787 (and under which the present government first went into operation,) and twelve subsequently framed amendments, the first ten of which were framed in 1789.

> Who were our fathers that framed the Constitution? I suppose the "thirty-nine" who signed the original instrument may be fairly called our fathers who framed that part of the present Government. It is almost exactly true to say they framed it, and it is altogether true to say they fairly represented the opinion and sentiment of the whole nation at that time. Their names, being familiar to nearly all, and accessible to quite all, need not be now repeated. (Lincoln 517–518)

Facts are assertions that speakers cannot imagine a competent person challenging. It is a fact that Senator Douglas made the remark Lincoln attributes to him; it is a fact that the Constitution was ratified in 1787 and later amended; it is a fact that there were thirty-nine signers of the Constitution. But it is a truth, not merely a fact, that that document *constitutes* our government, a truth that must be the basis of any views concerning the extention of slavery to the territories. Truths transcend, but are in conformity with the facts of the world. Current scientific theories are truths; so are political theories that explain and justify our form of government.

The speaker's idea of his audience must also include their idea of values, of the preferable.[1] To illustrate the components of the preferable, we will use the opening remarks in the fourth Lincoln-Douglas debate, in Charleston, Illinois, on September 18,1858. In his beginning, Lincoln rehearses values, hierarchies of values, and the loci of quality or quantity that establish or intensify these values, components of the preferable he believes he shares with his audience:

> While I was up at the hotel to-day, an elderly gentleman called upon me to know whether I was really in favor of producing a perfect equality between the negroes and the white people. While I had not proposed to myself upon this occasion to say much upon that subject, as the question was asked me, I thought I would occupy, perhaps, five minutes, in saying something in regard to it.
>
> I will say then, that I am not nor ever have been in favor of bringing about in any way, the social and political equality of the white and black races, that I am not, nor ever have been in favor of making voters of the negroes, or jurors, or qualifying them to hold office, or having them marry with white people. I will say in addition, that there is a physical difference between the white and black races, which I suppose will forever forbid the two races living together upon terms of social and political equality, and inasmuch, as they cannot so live, that while they do remain together, there must be the position of superior and inferior, that I as much as any other man am in favor of the superior position being assigned to the white man. I say in this connection, that I do not perceive, however, that because the white man is to have the superior position, that it requires that the negro

> should be denied everything. I do not perceive because I do not court a negro woman for a wife, that I must necessarily want her for a [slave]. My understanding is that I can just leave her alone. I am now in my fiftieth year, and certainly have never had a black woman either for a slave or wife, so that it seems to me that it is quite possible for us to get along without making either slaves or wives of negroes. (Lincoln-Douglas 189)

In this exordium, Lincoln assumes that he shares two values with the audience he imagines: the Constitutional imperative that all men are created equal, and the social and political imperative that blacks are inferior. These values he arranges in a hierarchy in which the Constitutional imperative has the priority—constrained, of course, by the social and political imperative of black inferiority as a justification for the denial of full citizenship.

Values and hierarchies of values may merely be asserted on the basis of authority, but they may also be justified by means of general schemes of inference, which Perelman and Olbrechts-Tyteca identify with the classical loci or topics. Important in this connection are the loci of quantity and quality. According to the first, the preferable is to be preferred because it provides *more* of a good; according to the second, it is to be preferred because the good it provides is *greater* than some other, lesser good. It is a locus of quality that anchors Lincoln's nuanced racism in his debate with Douglas: a physical difference that is, presumably, a sign of mental inferiority is thus reconciled with a document that insists all men are created equal. The locus of quantity is specifically sidestepped: it does not matter how many black Americans there are: none is entitled to full citizenship. Along with this neglect one aspect of the locus of quality is also avoided: even if the black race is generally inferior to the white, can it also be true that *every* black is inferior to *every* white?

The general inferiority of "negroes" is a presumption of Lincoln's argument. Presumptions are matters that can be taken for granted by speakers and audiences: the presumption of innocence, for example. This does not mean that particular defendants *are* innocent, only that they are innocent until proven guilty, that, in criminal proceedings, it is the state that bears the burden of proof. Analogously, Lincoln bears the burden of proof when he argues that the general inferiority of negroes does not imply that they have no rights whatever. He could not so argue if this inferiority was a fact or a truth. As Perelman and Olbrechts-Tyteca assert, presumptions are intimately connected with what audiences regard as normal: In addition, "the existence of this connection between presumptions and what is normal is itself a general presumption accepted by all audiences" (71). It is because presumption coincides with the normal that it fixes the burden of proof.

We next come to the puzzle of Perelman and Olbrechts-Tyteca's distinction between particular and universal audiences, a puzzle that can be solved now that we understand the difference between the real and the preferable. Since all rhetorical audiences are constructed, both particular and universal audiences are, equally, those imagined by the speaker. The difference is that speeches for the universal audience focus on the real; those for particular audiences focus on the preferable:

> The conceptions people form of the real can vary widely, depending on the philosophical views they profess. However, everything in argumentation that is deemed to relate to the real is characterized by a claim to validity vis-à-vis the universal audience. On the contrary, all that pertains to the preferable, that which determines our choices and does not conform to a preexistent reality, will be connected with a specific viewpoint which is necessarily identified with some particular audience, though it may be a large one. (66)

It is only in the former case, according to Perelman and Olbrechts-Tyteca, that the speaker is addressing a universal audience, that is, he is addressing the men and women actually before him, not as Americans or Republicans, as Catholics or Jews, but as rational human beings. He is presuming, through his argumentation, to convince, rather than to persuade,

> to gain the adherence of every rational being. The nuance involved is a delicate one and depends, essentially, on the idea the speaker has formed [of] the incarnation of reason. Every person believes a set of facts, of truths, which he thinks must be accepted by every "normal" person, because they are valid for every rational being. But is this really the case? Does not this claim to an absolute validity for any audience composed of rational beings go too far? On this point, even the most conscientious writer can do no more than submit to the test of facts, to his readers' judgment. In any case he will have done all he can to *convince*, if he thinks he is validly addressing such an audience. (28)

Clearly, at this point in our intellectual history it would be futile to argue that either philosophy or science is value-free. Perelman and Olbrechts-Tyteca's point, however, is not that such discourse is value-free, but that it is a condition for making philosophical and scientific assertions that they be addressed to an audience of all rational beings, namely, to a universal audience: "The thesis defended in *The New Rhetoric* is that every philosopher addresses himself to the universal audience *as he conceives it*, even in *the absence of an objectivity* which imposes itself on everyone. The philosopher develops an argumentation thanks to which he aspires to convince any competent interlocutor whatsover" ("The New Rhetoric," 191). The universal audience is an ideal that must be assumed in such discourse. Discourse that focuses on values can never address a universal audience because particular values can never be plausibly asserted as binding on all human beings in all circumstances.

We can now place Ede's criticism of the universal audience in its proper context. It is true that "argumentation addressed to the universal audience must convince the reader that the reasons adduced are of a compelling character, that they are self evident, and possess an absolute timeless validity, independent of local or historical contingencies" (32). But this is not because such timeless validity exists; rather, it is because speakers arguing for the real in a particular case must assume its existence in the general case. All such arguments are subject to the paradox that speakers must presuppose a concept of timeless validity, a concept clearly subject to contingency. As Perelman and Olbrechts-Tyteca put it: "Each individual, each culture, has thus its own conception of the universal audience" (33).

We can see this paradox clearly if we look at philosophy, for Perelman and Olbrechts-Tyteca paradigmatic of discourse addressed to a universal audience. To illustrate, we reproduce a speech of Socrates from Plato's dialogue, *Phaedrus*. In this section of the dialogue, Socrates addresses a single interlocutor, Phaedrus, as if he were a universal audience of rational beings. Socrates is outlining the conditions that a science of rhetoric must satisfy:

> SOCRATES. Since the nature of speech is in fact to direct the soul, whoever intends to be a rhetorician must know how many kinds of soul there are. Their number is so-and-so many; each is of such-and-such sort; hence some people have such-and-such character and others have such-and-such. Those distinctions established, there are, in turn, so-and-so many kinds of speech, each of such-and-such a sort. People of such-and-such a character are easy to persuade by speeches of such-and-such a sort in connection with such-and-such an issue for this particular reason, while people of such-and-such another sort are difficult to persuade for those particular reasons.
>
> The orator must learn all this well, then put his theory into practice and develop the ability to discern each kind clearly as it occurs in the actions of real life. Otherwise he won't be any better off than he was when he was still listening to those discussions in school. He will now not only be able to say what kind of person is convinced by what kind of speech; on meeting someone he will be able to discern what he is like and make clear to himself that the person actually standing in front of him is just this particular sort of character he had learned about in school—to that he must now apply

> speeches of such-and-such kind in this particular way in order to secure conviction about such-and-such an issue. When he has learned all this—when, in addition, he has grasped the right occasions for speaking and for holding back; and when he has also understood that the time is right for Speaking Concisely or Appealing to Pity or Exaggeration or any other of the kinds of speech he has learned and when it is not—then, and only then, will he have finally mastered the art well and completely. But if his speaking, his teaching, or his writing lacks any one of these elements and he still claims to be speaking with art, you'll be better off if you don't believe him. (Plato 271d-272b)

In this speech, we recognize the contingency of Socrates's views. Few today would accept Socrates's vision of a science of rhetoric, one that depends on a precise knowledge of the constitution of particular "souls." At the same time, the *Phaedrus* is philosophical discourse, discourse in which Socrates imagines every member of his audience as a rational being, an embodiment of universal standards of rationality. It is this view of audience that accounts for the emphasis in philosophical discourse on logical as distinct from emotional appeals. It accounts also for the absence of symbols in such discourse, symbols which, like the flag or the eagle, are "characteristic of a particular culture" (335).[2] While philosophy is Perelman and Olbrechts-Tyteca's paradigm for discourse addressed to a universal audience, their definition applies as well to all scholarly discourse, including their own work.

Another sort of discourse that addresses the universal audience is that of the sciences. Like philosophy, it participates in the apparent paradox that, while there is an actual audience of real people, the audience the speaker addresses is universal: "The scientist addresses himself to certain peculiarly qualified men, who accept the data of a well-defined system consisting of the science in which they are specialists. Yet, this very limited audience is generally considered by the scientist to be really the universal audience, and not just a particular audience. He supposes that everyone with the same training, qualifications, and information would reach the same conclusions" (34). To illustrate the universal audience addressed by scientists, we cite a passage from the *Almagest* of Ptolemy, the great ancient astronomer. Ptolemy is arguing for the immobility of the earth at the center of the universe:

> If the earth had a single motion in common with other heavy objects, it is obvious that it would be carried down faster than all of them because of its much greater size: living things and individual heavy objects would be left behind, riding on the air, and the earth itself would very soon have fallen

> completely out of the heavens. But such things are utterly ridiculous merely to think of. (p. 44)

No one today would find Ptolemy's argument compelling, since no one today would presuppose the Aristotelian physics that Ptolemy presupposes. But the fact that this passage is, from our point of view, riddled with errors does not affect the fact that Ptolemy was addressing a universal audience with what he thought were compelling arguments, arguments so compelling that he believed that those who would disagree with him had a burden of proof so heavy that it was "ridiculous" to try to discharge it.

Let us now turn from these relatively "pure" cases of discourse in the sciences and philosophy—each in its own way addressed to a universal audience—to the mixed discourse of public address, discourse Perelman and Olbrechts-Tyteca refrain from analyzing. Let us look at Lincoln's reply to Douglas at Galesburg, on October 7, 1858:

> I suppose that the real difference between Judge Douglas and his friends, on the one side, and the Republicans on the other hand is, that the Judge is not in favor of making any difference between slavery and liberty, that he is in favor of eradicating, he is in favor of pressing out of view, and out of existence, all preference for free over slave institutions, and, consequently, every sentiment that he utters, discards the idea that he is against slavery, every sentiment that emanates from him discards the idea that there is any wrong in slavery. Every thought that he utters will be seen to exclude the thought that there is anything wrong in slavery. You will take his speeches and get the short pointed sentiments expressed by him, that he does not care if slavery is voted up, or voted down, and such like, you will see at once that it is a perfectly logical idea if you admit that slavery is not wrong, but if it is wrong, Judge Douglas cannot say that he don't care for a wrong being voted up. Judge Douglas declares that if any community wants slavery they can have it. He can logically say that, if he admits that there is no wrong in it, but he cannot say that, if he admits that there is wrong in it! He insists, upon the score of equality, that the owner of slaves and the owner of horses should be allowed to take them alike to new territory and hold them there. That is perfectly logical if the species of property is perfectly alike, but if you admit that one of them is wrong, then you cannot admit any equality between right and wrong. I believe that slavery is wrong, and in a policy springing from that belief that looks to the prevention of the enlargement of that wrong, and that looks at some time to there being an end of that wrong. The other sentiment is, that there is no wrong, and the policy springing from it that there is no wrong in its becoming bigger, and that there never will be any end of it. There is the difference between Judge Douglas and his friends and the Republican party. (Lincoln-Douglas 257–258)

We think that such discourse is typical of public address in that while arguments of value are primary, arguments of fact are also evident. In so far as Lincoln is arguing for the fact that Douglas has certain views, views that have definite ethical consequences, he is speaking to his audience at Galesburg as if they were the universal audience. Whether or not Douglas holds these views, and whether or not these views have these consequences are matters of fact and truth. But Lincoln is also discoursing about values. He is asserting slavery is wrong and that Douglas is wrong to endorse it. In arguing about values, Lincoln is addressing a particular audience, though one might more truly say, particular audiences, since the Galesburg audience is long dead, and his words speak to us as well, another particular audience. As wide as this audience may have been in Lincoln's time, however, as wide as it may be over time, nevertheless it does not represent every rational human being.

Perelman and Olbrechts-Tyteca feel that in all persuasive discourse the audience alters in character as the discourse progresses. Of course, it is still, at the end of discourse, what it was at the beginning, a construction of the speaker. But it is a construction that has altered as a consequence of the degree to which the speaker feels that he has advanced the adherence of the audience he imagines from their initial views to those he would prefer them to have. This means that for the universal, as for the particular audience, the order of discourse is crucial:

> A speech does not leave the hearer the same as he was at the beginning. On the other hand, it does not change his beliefs irresistibly, as would the steps in a demonstration. If it did, order would not be of such importance. The order adopted is crucial precisely because the changes in the audience are both effective and contingent.
>
> This is true of the different incarnations of the universal audience as it is of particular audiences. At first sight, order does not matter to the universal audience. But the universal audience is no less than other audiences a concrete audience, which changes with time, along with the speaker's conception of it. (491)

We can see change in the speaker's conception of his audience in operation by examining the beginning and ending of Lincoln's First Inaugural:

> Fellow-citizens of the United States:
>
> In compliance with a custom as old as the government itself, I appear before you to address you briefly, and to take, in your presence, the oath prescribed by the Constitution of the United States, to be taken by the President "before he enters on the execution of his office."

> I do not consider it necessary at present for me to discuss those matters of administration about which there is no special anxiety or excitement.
>
> Apprehension seems to exist among the people of the Southern States, that by the accession of a Republican Administration, their property, and their peace, and personal security, are to be endangered. There has never been any reasonable cause for such apprehension. Indeed, the most ample evidence to the contrary has all the while existed, and has been open to their inspection. It is found in nearly all the published speeches of him who now addresses you. I do but quote from one of those speeches when I declare that "I have no purpose, directly or indirectly, to interfere with the institution of slavery in the States where it exists. I believe I have no lawful right to do so, and I have no inclination to do so." Those who nominated and elected me did so with full knowledge that I had made this, and many similar declarations, and had never recanted them.
>
> . . . .
>
> In *your* hands, my dissatisfied fellow countrymen, and not in *mine*, is the momentous issue of civil war. The government will not assail *you*. You can have no conflict, without being yourself the aggressors. *You* have no oath registered in Heaven to destroy the government, while *I* shall have the most solemn one to "preserve, protect and defend" *it*.
>
> I am loath to close. We are not enemies, but friends. We must not be enemies. Though passion may have strained, it must not break our bonds of affection. The mystic chords of memory, stretching from every battle-field, and patriot grave, to every living heart and hearth-stone, all over this broad land, will yet swell the chorus of the Union, when again touched, as surely they will be, by the better angels of our nature. (Lincoln 579–88)

The rhetorical audience at the end of Lincoln's address is very different from the one that forms its starting point. At the beginning of his speech, Lincoln assumes only that he must calm Southern apprehensions concerning his election by producing facts and arguments that clarify his resolve not to interfere with slavery in the South. Only when he has accomplished this task in the body of his speech does he feel justified in arguing for the preservation of the Union. Only after these latter arguments are completed does he attempt the direct emotional appeals to the South with which he ends. These final appeals cannot work unless the South's apprehensions have seriously and substantially diminished.

We may summarize by saying that Perelman and Olbrechts-Tyteca have a complete and coherent theory of a rhetorical audience as a concept constructed by the speaker. This audience is of two kinds, universal and particular. Universal audiences consist of all rational beings; persuasive discourse addressed to these make facts, truths, and presumptions central. Philosophy and science are examples of such discourse. Particular audiences consist of one segment or another of humanity: Americans, Republicans, Elks, Medicare recipients; discourse addressed to them makes values central. Public address is a paradigm of such discourse. But discourse in public arenas is rarely addressed simply to particular audiences or to a universal audience; it rarely has as its goal *either* adherence to facts, truths, and presumptions *or* adherence to values. Usually, public address represents a mixture of goals, and therefore of rhetorical audiences. Finally, in all persuasive discourse, the concept of audience with which speakers start differs from the concept with which speakers end the discourse. By means of the discourse, step-by-step, speakers bring their rhetorical audience to the desired adherence; at the same time, they hope that their discourse brings their actual audience—the real people outside the realm of Perelmanian rhetorical theory—to the same point.

CHAPTER 4

Arguing Quasi-Logically

Now that we have scrutinized the philosophical underpinnings of Perelman's rhetorical thought and have analyzed the concept of rhetorical audience lying at its core, we are ready to examine the typology of argumentation set forth in *The New Rhetoric.* After discussing facts, truths, presumptions, and other "starting points" upon which arguments can be constructed, Perelman and Olbrechts-Tyteca proceed to explain the discursive techniques used by arguers to elicit agreements or "adherences" from their audiences. Arguments are sometimes structured in the form of an *association,* or liaison, in which the adherence accorded the premise is transferred to the conclusion; at other times, arguments are presented in the form of a *dissociation,* which seeks to persuade or convince an audience by separating elements of thought that were previously tied together, either by language or by a recognized tradition.

As we saw in Chapter 2, Perelman's early investigations in the 1930s, when he was still "imbued with positivism," revealed that beneath all knowledge claims lie axioms that cannot be postulated as self-evident, and whose selection cannot entirely escape the charge of arbitrariness. Furthermore, his analyses of logical fallacies, conducted from the same rationalistic paradigm, led him to conclude that formal logic—the only logic practiced by contemporary logicians—had become largely irrelevant to all practical reasoning about human affairs. Even as he came to this conclusion, Perelman recognized that the *notion of logic* continues to exert a powerful sway over the modern mind. To charge one's opponent with being "illogical" is to hurl a stinging rebuke, one that invites an immediate denial or rebuttal. This occurs in philosophical circles, courtroom settings, or even in conversations around the family dinner table. Presenting one's own arguments as "logical," on the other hand, goes a long way toward assuring them a favorable hearing.

If logic is indeed irrelevant to practical decision-making, how is it that its attraction remains so psychologically compelling? Perelman and Olbrechts-Tyteca scoured the logic books in vain, looking for a resolution to this dilemma. Finally, their extensive field investigations of argumentative practices yielded the solution, which appeared in the form of a species of arguments exhibiting a peculiar rhetorical property: these arguments owe their potency to their similarity to well-established formal structures. "Quasi-logical arguments," as the Belgian researchers dubbed them, "lay claim to a certain power of conviction in the degree that they claim to be similar to the formal reasoning of logic or mathematics" (*The New Rhetoric* 193). Any similarity between these arguments and formal reasoning, however, turns out to be purely illusory, as any careful analysis will reveal. As a case in point, take the following argument, which resembles a logically valid syllogism:

> Conservatives support the preservation of the *status quo*.
> Jones is a conservative.
> Hence, Jones supports the existing policies of the present administration.

Unlike a chain of formal reasoning, this argument contains terms that are not univocal. The term *status quo* in the major premise cannot be equated with the "policies of the present administration" in the conclusion, nor is the term "conservative" defined precisely enough to carry the same denotation in both premises. (In logic, this is known as the fallacy of the "undistributed middle.") Without putting too fine a point on the matter, we can say that this argument has a superficial plausibility, owing in part to its resemblance to the familiar logical pattern of deduction. But even a cursory examination shows it cannot meet the tests of formal validity.

Because an arguer seeks the adherence of an audience, not formal validity, however, his or her goal is not to establish a chain of reasoning in which some ideas are derived from others according to accepted rules of inference. "The quasi-logical argument's lack of rigor and preciseness may seem to be a logical flaw," writes Perelman, "but to charge a person with using a logically flawed argument would make sense only if that person claimed to advance a logical demonstration" (*Realm of Rhetoric* 53). Quasi-logical arguments are not simply deceptive or imprecise versions of the real thing; they are neither correct nor incorrect, but are weaker or stronger, depending upon how well they are reinforced by other kinds of arguments. Instead of relying on a chain of reasoning, argumentation consists of "a web formed from all the arguments and all the reasons that combine to achieve the desired result" (*The New Rhetoric and the Humanities* 18). With this principle in mind, let's see how the individual strands of this web can be spun out of resemblances to "well-known" principles of logical and mathematical reasoning.

Of all the possible relations on which arguments may be based, Perelman and Olbrechts-Tyteca discuss and illustrate certain ones that depend on logical relations—contradiction, total or partial identity, transitivity—and others that are based upon mathematical relations—the connection between the part and the whole, the smaller and the larger, frequency, and so forth. The chosen examples "can be understood and analyzed differently by different hearers and logical structures can be regarded as mathematical, and *vice versa*" (*The New Rhetoric* 194). The arguments in the remainder of this chapter, whether originally presented by Perelman and his co-author or added by the present authors, are specifically selected in order to highlight their quasi-logical character.

Contradiction and Incompatibility

The similarities and distinctions between logic and argumentation are brought sharply into focus by a close examination of contradiction and its rhetorical counterpart, incompatibility. Logic, as we recall, exists within a framework of preassigned conventions; it employs univocal terms and stipulated rules of inference. This being the case, whenever a contradiction is found, the chain of reasoning is rendered invalid. By contrast, argumentation uses premises that are inexplicit, and "it is permissible only in exceptional cases . . . to claim the presence of a contradiction in an opponent's system. Usually the line of argument tries to show that the theses one is disputing lead to an *incompatibility*, which resembles a contradiction in that it consists of two assertions between which a choice must be made . . ." (196). Inconsistency is intolerable in closed systems of thought, but argumentation unfolds over time and uses stratagems such as fiction, falsehood, or even silence to avoid inconsistency.

Sometimes the simple expedient of allowing time to pass is sufficient to avoid confronting the incompatibility. Consider the following argument framed as a logical deduction:

> We agreed that those who have doubts must withdraw. Well, Gerard has doubts.

> So from that it follows that Gerard must withdraw. Doesn't it? (van Eemeren *et al.* 231)

When we subject this line of reasoning to analysis, its quasi-logical character becomes evident. Circumstances might have changed since the original "agreement" was voiced. The nature of Gerard's "doubts" could be different from the kind of misgivings originally envisaged. It is even possible that the interlocutors would rather ignore the ostensible agreement than have Gerard withdraw. For Gerard to remain might seem incompatible with the prior decision, but it is far from logically contradictory for him to remain.

In a similar line of reasoning, Judge Stephen A. Douglas sought to impale his opponent, Abraham Lincoln, on the horns of a dilemma in their second joint debate at Freeport, Illinois, on August 27, 1858. Douglas seized upon Lincoln's Springfield speech in which he had argued that agitation on the slavery question would continue until the issue had been resolved. "A house divided against itself cannot stand," Lincoln had said, adding, "I believe this Government cannot endure permanently half slave and half free." Douglas continued:

> . . . Mr. Lincoln lays down the doctrine that this nation cannot endure divided as our fathers made it into free and slave states. He says they must all become one way or all the other—must all become free or all become slave, otherwise the Union cannot continue to exist. That being the case in his opinion, if we have any more Slave States, so that it would continue to be divided, it would dissolve the Union. . . . I want to know whether Mr. Lincoln will vote for another Slave State, believing that the effect of it will be to dissolve the Union? . . . The true intent and inevitable conclusion from his Springfield speech is, that he is opposed to the admission of any more Slave States under any circumstances. (*Lincoln-Douglas* 123–124)

By treating Lincoln's assertion as a logical argument involving two mutually exclusive alternatives, Douglas tried to place Lincoln in the position of either opposing the admission of a single new slave state or inviting the dissolution of the union. Lincoln, on the other hand, had spoken of an incompatibility rather than a logical contradiction. The Biblical allusion of the "house divided" had quasi-logical overtones that could not be refuted by objections based upon the canons of formal validity found in logic books.

Recognizing that incompatibility rather than contradiction is the proper charge to be leveled against inconsistencies in quasi-logical arguments, we can see how the technique of ridicule works in argumentation. "It is the ridiculous and not the absurd which is the principal weapon of argumentation," say Perelman and Olbrechts-Tyteca (*The New Rhetoric* 205). Ridicule usually involves the unconscious violation or opposition of a rule. We are reminded of the role played by the "rule of justice" in all rational activity: "Ridicule works toward the preservation of what is accepted; a simple unwarranted change in opinion . . . makes the speaker liable to ridicule" (206). The usual form of quasi-logical argumentation based upon ridicule consists of temporarily accepting a statement contradictory to what one actually wishes to defend, then deducing from it consequences that are patently incompatible with what is accepted on other grounds. Richard Whately used this technique in an anonymous pamphlet: "He began by admitting as established the kind of objections raised against the truth of the Scriptures and, by developing the consequences, he arrived at a denial of the existence of Napoleon" (207).

Identity

Arguments based upon total or partial identity include definitions that claim to identify (equate) the defining expression (*definiens*) with the term to be defined (*definiendum*). When "justice" is defined as treating people according to their "works," for example, the relation of identity that is posited by the definition is not formally valid, but is merely asserted by the speaker. Except in rare cases involving neologisms or scientific words with fixed meanings, all arguments using definitions are quasi-logical. They attempt to transfer to the *definiens* the value attributed to the *definiendum*. Whether the interchangeability is accepted is a matter of audience adherence, not logical validity.

Another species of arguments based upon the relation of identity includes those that appear to be analytic or tautological. When analysis is used in argumentation, it is never strictly logical; it is invariably directed toward securing an interlocutor's agreement. So long as one says, "A is the child of B," the expression can logically be taken to mean "A is the son or daughter of B." But when we read that "John Quincy Adams was truly Abigail Adams' son," we look for a subtler meaning, perhaps one involving personality features or character traits. We suspect in any case that the writer is hinting at something that transcends genealogy, so we search in the surrounding context for added clues to the statement's signification.

In like manner, genuine tautologies hardly ever arise in argument. Whenever we hear expressions such as "Business is business," "A penny is a penny," or "Boys will be boys," we implicitly understand that a formal identity is asserted between two terms that cannot really be identical if the statement is to be of interest (*The New Rhetoric* 217). Tautologies are quasi-logical because, at first glance, the terms seem univocal and capable of being identified, whereas differences arise after interpretation. The identities asserted in argumentation, Perelman believed, are never complete; they depend upon the context for their meaning, and the reader or hearer bears part of the responsibility for their interpretation.

Other quasi-logical arguments are based on "reciprocal relations." "What is honorable to learn is also honorable to teach," argued Quintilian. And La Bruyère insisted that if actors are to be condemned for performing in plays, the Christians who attend them should also be condemned. Based on the connection between the antecedent and the consequent, these arguments by reciprocity seem to be "at once formal and based on the nature of things" (221).

Transitivity

The final group of arguments modeled after logical relationships is based on transitivity, "a formal property of certain relationships which makes it possible to infer that because a relation holds between *a* and *b* and between *b* and *c*, it therefore holds between *a* and *c*" (221). The relations of equality, superiority, inclusion, and ancestry are transitive in nature. Rhetorical forms such as the *enthymeme* and *epichirema* are usually based upon one of these relations, which in turn mimics the syllogistic form found in logic. For example, the well-known syllogism

> All men are mortal.
> Socrates is a man.
> Therefore, Socrates is mortal.

rests upon the transitive principle of inclusion. (Socrates is included within the category of men, hence of mortals.)

Often when arguments appearing to be logically ironclad are subjected to analysis, their quasi-logical character is revealed. Perelman and Olbrechts-Tyteca write:

> The transitivity of a relation allows formal demonstrations, but when the transitivity is debatable, or when affirming it requires precautions, [or] specification, the transitivity argument is structurally quasi-logical. Thus the maxim, "Our friends' friends are our friends," really involves an assertion

> that in the mind of the person proclaiming the maxim, friendship is a transitive relation. If objections are raised—based on observation or on an analysis of the concept of friendship—the defender of the maxim can always reply that this is his conception of true friendship and that true friends ought to act in conformity to the maxim. (227)

In brief review, arguments based on contradiction, identity, or transitivity are never strictly formal. They derive their force (in part, at least) from their similarity to well-recognized structures of rigorous logic. In every case, the differences between logic and argumentation—the association of the former with a closed system utilizing predetermined instruments and defined procedures, and of the latter with an open system subject to temporality and using language that is seldom univocal—account for the quasi-logical nature of these arguments.

Mathematical Relations

Let us now turn to the class of quasi-logical arguments in which a mathematical relation is claimed or implicitly posited. This group includes structures of thought such as inclusion (used quantitatively, as when a whole is equated with the sum of its parts); division (when the parts are considered as subdivisions of the whole); comparisons (involving weights and measures); and probabilities of all sorts.

At first glance, the distinction between arguments of inclusion and those of division might not be obvious. For a specimen of the former kind of reasoning, we may turn to an argument advanced by John Locke: "For whatsoever is not lawful to the whole Church cannot by any ecclesiastical right become lawful to any of its members" (231). Here the Church is assumed to be composed of its parts or members, which are deemed similar to the whole body, at least insofar as their legal obligations are concerned. An argument by division, on the other hand, is apparent in the following argument adduced by Aristotle: "All men do wrong from one of three motives: *A*, *B*, or *C*; in my case *A* and *B* are out of the question, and even the accusers do not allege *C*" (234). This argument is not purely formal, because "it requires a knowledge of the relations which the parts actually have with the particular case under consideration" (235). In other words, the audience is asked to believe that all possible motives for wrongdoing have been exhausted in the opening premise. Once that is granted, a simple mathematical elimination leads to the desired conclusion.

A glaring distinction between arguments of inclusion and those of division shows up in the recurring and intractable debate over the relationship between the federal government of the United States and its respective states. From the earliest days of the Republic, parties divided over this question, the Federalists holding that the national authority is supreme over the states, which are viewed as logically subordinate (as parts of a whole) to the central government. By contrast, Republicans (as Jeffersonians were then known) held that the states, having entered into a compact to create the federal union, are logically superior to their "creature." As separate entities, not as "parts of a whole," the states were believed to retain their sovereignty over matters not specifically assigned by the Constitution to the federal government. The Tenth Amendment to the Constitution appeared to support this interpretation: "The powers not delegated to the United States by the Constitution, nor prohibited by it to the States, are reserved to the States respectively, or to the people."

Upon the basis of the latter interpretation of the federal-state relationship, proponents of "states' rights" were arguing by the end of the 1820s that individual states had the power to "nullify" within their own borders a federal law deemed repugnant by its inhabitants. Thus, Senator John C. Calhoun of South Carolina bitterly denounced the imposition of a federal tariff, the so-called "Tariff of Abominations," arguing that the national government had exceeded its constitutional authority. After quoting the Tenth Amendment, Calhoun said, "The Government is thus positively restricted to the exercise of those general powers that were supposed to act uniformly on the parts,—leaving the residue to the people of the States, by whom . . . they can be justly and fairly exercised . . ." (Reid 273–274). On another issue—the sale of Western lands by the U.S. government—South Carolina's other senator, Robert Y. Hayne, brought the issue of nullification to the forefront of national attention early in 1830. To bolster his case, Hayne invoked the authority of two preeminent constitutional authors, James Madison and Thomas Jefferson. He quoted Jefferson's opinion, expressed in 1821, that, "It is a fatal heresy to suppose that either our State governments are superior to the Federal, or the Federal to the State; neither is authorized literally to decide which belongs to itself or its copartner in government" (Reid 283).

During the course of the Western lands dispute in the Senate, Daniel Webster of Massachusetts spoke in reply to Hayne's arguments. Webster conceded that the Constitution had left certain powers to the states, but he argued that "The people of the United States shall be the supreme law," that "the General Government and the State governments derive their authority from the same source," and that "the people of the United States have chosen to impose control on State sovereignties" (Reid 291–292). Webster's view that the nation was not divisible into twenty-four separate sovereignties (the number of the existing states) was expressed in his stirring peroration: "Liberty and Union, now and forever one and inseparable!" (310).

The Civil War of 1861–1865 appeared to settle by a clash of arms the question as to whether the United States was "one nation indivisible" or a confederation of semi-autonomous states; yet the rhetorical battle continued to rage throughout the nineteenth and twentieth centuries. Although the powers of the federal government were increasingly upheld by the Supreme Court during most of the latter half of the twentieth century, the trend had abated somewhat by the 1990s, when, for example, the Court held that a federal law mandating that local law enforcement officers conduct background checks on purchasers of handguns was ruled unconstitutional on the basis of the Tenth Amendment. Is the United States to be viewed as a sovereign authority exercising supremacy over its states, which are regarded as "parts of a whole"; or is it a "summation" of the various states, each of which retains sovereignty over matters within its own jurisdiction? In a sense, the dispute is as lively as it was during the Webster-Hayne debates of 1830. However one approaches this question, the ensuing argument will be *quasi*-logical; its effectiveness will depend not upon actual mathematical principles or calculations but upon its capacity to bring about a confirmation or alteration in the thinking of an audience.

One final example of arguments that rely on quasi-mathematical relations should suffice: "Arguments by comparison are quasi-logical. They are often presented as a statement of fact, whereas the relation of equality or inequality which is asserted is often nothing more than a claim of the speaker" (*The New Rhetoric* 242). Even when a quantitative assertion is strictly true, it can have differing rhetorical effects, depending upon the basis chosen for the comparison. Generally speaking, it is better to be compared with someone of impeccable esteem, even if one falls short, than to be compared with an inferior whom one is said to surpass in some way. As an exception to the rule, it sounds more impressive to French citizens to "describe a country as nine times larger than France rather than half as large as Brazil" (245).

The quasi-logical arguments examined by Perelman and Olbrechts-Tyteca cannot be pigeonholed into discrete categories. Whether such devices are based on logical relations—contradiction, total or partial identity, transitivity—or depend on mathematical relations—the part and the whole, the smaller and the larger, frequency, etc.—they "can be understood and analyzed differently by different hearers, and logical structures can be regarded as mathematical and *vice versa*" (*The New Rhetoric* 194). Readers familiar with Aristotle's *Rhetoric* might classify Webster's argument for a strong federal union as simply a variation of the "line of argument" (*topos*) known as "the greater and the lesser" (1363b 6–11). However one chooses to label them, these arguments do not exhibit the rigor associated with valid logic; their formal or quantitative aspects are muted and escape the notice of all but the most acute readers or hearers. Even though the source of their appeal is unobtrusive—perhaps even subliminal—these arguments display similarities to familiar patterns of logic, and, if Perelman and Olbrechts-Tyteca are correct, this quasi-logical character contributes to their persuasiveness. Seldom, however, do they carry conviction by themselves; usually they must be supplemented by other forms of reasoning, including arguments based on the structure of reality.

CHAPTER 5

Arguing from the Structure of Reality

Unlike quasi-logical arguments, which try to counterfeit logical or mathematical structures, a second kind of associative technique relies upon the audience's conception of reality in order "to establish a solidarity between accepted judgments and others which one wishes to promote" (*The New Rhetoric* 261). The purpose of this chapter is to explore the nature of these arguments and determine how they fit into Perelman's rhetorical enterprise.

We must stipulate at the outset that Perelman's personal ontological and epistemological views are not germane to the present inquiry; his rejection of both the "realist" and "nominalist" positions was documented in an earlier chapter; and it could be added that in none of the writings we have examined does Perelman either posit or reject the existence of a "purely objective" reality apart from human experience. From the rhetorical rather than the philosophical standpoint, however, as F. H. van Eemeren and his colleagues interpret the Belgian philosopher as saying, any speaker basing an argumentation on the structure of reality "will be bent on making his [or her] audience believe that he [or she] is presenting an *inevitable* picture of reality" (van Eemeren *et al.* 234). Such a view of reality would be antithetical, of course, to Perelman's regressive philosophy, which holds that even the facts, truths, and presumptions upon which a view of reality is based consist only of "the best tested of our opinions"; and it bears repeating that all argumentation is predicated upon the belief system of the intended audience.

It should also be reiterated that individual arguments cannot always be confined to single, discrete categories in Perelman's typology. As we have just seen, quasi-logical arguments *sometimes* mimic the pattern known as deduction. Yet the arguments to be examined presently are also based upon the syllogistic principle whereby a conclusion is deduced from a particular view of reality (i.e., a major premise) already accepted by the audience. If the notion that "all men are mortal" were not firmly embedded in human consciousness, the famous conclusion concerning Socrates's mortality would not be psychologically compelling. It is not at all inconsistent (or incompatible, as Perelman would prefer to say) to maintain that such a pattern of reasoning is both quasi-logical and is based upon the existing worldview of an audience. With this caveat in mind, let us look closely at two kinds of liaisons that connect judgments already accepted by an audience with those the speaker wants to establish.

Sequential Relations

Arguments built upon liaisons of succession correspond to the area of logic traditionally termed "causal reasoning," which involves the forging of connections between events or phenomena that occur in a temporal sequence. Into this group Perelman and Olbrechts-Tyteca place the "pragmatic argument" (which evaluates an act or event on the basis of its consequences); arguments concerning ends and means; and the arguments of "waste," "direction," and "unlimited development."

When pragmatic arguments are used, a speaker tries to draw conclusions about the existence or value of a thing by evaluating it in terms of its favorable or unfavorable consequences. In effect, the arguer seeks to transfer the positive or negative opinions an audience holds toward an act or circumstance to the agent or condition alleged to have caused it. During the 1930s, for example, Senator Huey P. Long of Louisiana relied heavily on pragmatic argumentation to inveigh against the scandalous maldistribution of wealth in the United States. Between the "haves" and "have-nots" a great chasm yawned, a condition that, as Long insisted, caused millions to struggle in poverty while a few lived in splendid luxury. In a radio broadcast on February 23, 1934, the senator hurled blast after blast against the ten or twelve economic titans who, he declared, had accumulated more individual wealth than the other 120 million Americans combined:

> The greed of a few men is such that they think it is necessary that they own everything, and their pleasure consists in the starvation of the masses, and in their possessing things they cannot use, and their children cannot use, but who bask in the splendor of sunlight and wealth, casting darkness and despair and impressing it on everyone else. (Ryan 39)

The Great Depression constituted an unquestioned calamity—an economic certitude of the highest order—for Long's radio listeners on that winter night; and upon that reality he sought to create a causal linkage in their minds between this condition and the stockpiling of vast fortunes by the Morgans and Rockefellers, his ultimate goal being the radical restructuring of the nation's social reality.

As in the case of pragmatic argumentation, the sequential relationship existing between *means* and *end* is deemed to be causal whenever an event or circumstance is brought about through deliberate human action. This species of arguments works by transferring the audience's view of a given means to its corresponding end. This was the tack taken by the Virginia lawyer Patrick Henry on March 23, 1775, when he introduced a resolution to raise a militia and adopt a posture of defense in the face of British military maneuvers. To the assembled delegates to the Virginia Convention, Henry pointed to the "warlike preparations" being mounted by the British:

> Are fleets and armies necessary to a work of love and reconciliation? Have we shown ourselves so unwilling to be reconciled, that force must be called in to win back our love? Let us not deceive ourselves, sir. These are the implements of war and subjugation; the last arguments to which kings resort. I ask gentlemen, sir, what means this martial array, if its purpose be not to force us to submission? Can gentlemen assign any other possible motives for it? Has Great Britain any enemy, in this quarter of the world, to call for all this accumulation of navies and armies? No, sir, she has none. They are meant for us; they can be meant for no other. They are sent over to bind and rivet upon us those chains which the British ministry have been so long forging. (Baird 30–31)

The proximate threats to American freedom posed by the British vessels and armies were unquestionably real to the Virginians gathered in Richmond, and upon this reality Henry created a vital connection in a chain of logic leading to his celebrated "liberty or death" peroration.

By spinning the means-end relation on its axis, one can create an argument based upon the idea of *waste*. Abraham Lincoln used this line of reasoning when he lamented that the Army of the Potomac languished in its bivouac for several months during the first year of the Civil War while its moody, indecisive commander failed to act. The exasperated President confided to an adviser that, "if McClellan did not want to use the army, he [Lincoln] would like to borrow it" (Sandburg I, 418). To avoid wasting accumulated resources or effort, it seems necessary to press on until the end is achieved. Because of the sacrifice already made, the same rationale is "given by the banker who continues to lend to an insolvent debtor in the hope of getting him on his feet again in the long run" (*The New Rhetoric* 279). By putting a particular twist on the argument of waste, one can subsume under it all lines of thought that stress the need to avoid missing an opportunity, to strike while the iron is hot, or to utilize rare and irreplaceable assets, of which time is the most precious. "Dost thou love life? Then do not squander time; for that's the stuff life is made of," admonished Benjamin Franklin in *Poor Richard's Almanac* (Franklin 298). In the same vein, Emerson counseled the graduating seniors at Harvard in 1832:

> Man Thinking must not be subdued by his instruments. Books are for the scholar's idle times. When he can read God directly, the hour is too precious to be wasted in other men's transcripts of their readings. But when the intervals of darkness come, as come they must,—when the sun is hid and the stars withdraw their shining,—we repair to the lamps which were kindled by their ray, to guide our steps to the East again, where the dawn is. (Baird 127)

In the timeless realm of formal logic, there would be no need to employ the argument of waste, but we are reminded again that all argumentation takes place in a world bounded by temporality on every side.

Real arguments likewise occur in a spatial frame of reference. The argument of *direction* warns against the unforeseen hazards of pursuing a course of thought or action indefinitely. It consists, in its negative form, of guarding against the "device of stages": "If you give in this time, you will have to give in a little more next time, and heaven knows where you will stop" (*The New Rhetoric* 282). The structure of reality is pictured as a series of steps leading to disaster. By contrast, the arguer who refutes an argument of direction starts out with a decidedly different conception of reality and devises any of several possible replies: instead of a slippery slope, the predicament is depicted as a succession of stages in which the first step does not necessarily lead to the next, or qualitative differences exist among the various stages, or perhaps it is necessary to take the first step so as to be able to stop before the next is reached. When clear-cut phases or increments can be identified, such a rebuttal stands a good chance of succeeding. However, when the progression of evil or disease is presented as intrinsically organic, the argument of direction is harder to deflect or refute. The idea that a rotten apple, left alone, will spoil the whole barrel, or that an untreated cancer will eventually destroy the whole body, is thoroughly engrained in popular thought.

Occasionally arguments based upon a notion of the real make use of discrete, quantitative changes in order to effect a gradual qualitative alteration of the reality itself. In *The Realm of Rhetoric*, Perelman asks:

> At what moment does change become no longer one of degree but one of nature? At what point does taxation become confiscation? At what moment does the nationalization of entire branches of industry transform the economy of a country into a socialist one? This discussion is only a variant of the method of stages, wherein each stage is of a quantitative nature, but the end result may become qualitative change, a change of nature. (89)

Unlike the argument of direction, which expresses dread at the prospect of continuing a course of action indefinitely, the argument of *unlimited development* sees nothing but good ahead; the stepping-stone to disaster becomes a springboard to a bright and boundless future. The person who refutes such an argument stresses that all good things (save virtue itself, perhaps, which Aristotle makes the sole exception) can be carried to an extreme: freedom and order, for example, are positive values but become incompatible at some point when they collide with each other. In Perelman's view, two rhetorical figures, *hyperbole* and *litotes*, serve the purposes of unlimited development by exaggerating or minimizing a direction of thought. In Chapter 9 we shall examine the argumentative uses of these and other figures, which theorists before Perelman had treated almost entirely as techniques of stylistic embellishment.

Coexistential Relations

Besides the associative techniques predicated on sequential relations, there are others based simply on liaisons of coexistence. The common textbook fallacy expressed as *post hoc, ergo propter hoc* warns that things occurring together in time are not necessarily causally related. Yet certain connections seem inherently real, and from them convincing inferences can be drawn.

The prototypical relation of coexistence is the act-person connection. Seven years before *The New Rhetoric* was published, Perelman and Olbrechts-Tyteca scrutinized this relationship at great length in their article "Act and Person in Argument." Even at that early juncture in their collaboration, it was clear that rhetorical—not just philosophical—questions were beginning to drive the Belgians' research agenda. The following passage foreshadowed the role this seminal concept would come to play in the New Rhetoric:

> One of the connections of coexistence which may be considered as very generally accepted by all sorts of audiences and which seem to us to have a great importance is that of the relation of the person to the act which is attributed

> to him, a relation which is the prototype of a large number of connections of coexistence.
>
> The makeup of the human person and its separation from his acts is tied to a distinction between what is considered important, natural, and characteristic of the being under discussion and what is regarded as a transitory and external manifestation thereof. The makeup of the person always gives us a rule, in virtue of which the essence may be distinguished from its manifestations. ("Act and Person" 253)

In the act-person relationship, the "act" can be broadly interpreted to mean any "emanation" of the person, not simply actions but "judgments, modes of expression, emotional reactions, or involuntary mannerisms" (256).

The reality experienced by different audiences varies considerably from one time period or culture or philosophical system to another. By 1958 when their major work on argumentation appeared, Perelman and Olbrechts-Tyteca had embraced an even more expansive notion of both "act" and "person." "The argumentation of primitive people would use a much wider concept of the person than ours," they wrote in the Eurocentric idiom of the time. "They would doubtless include in it all its *appurtenances*, such as shadow, totem, name, and detached fragments of the body, whereas we would establish only a symbolic connection between these elements and the totality of the person" (*The New Rhetoric* 293). However widely interpreted, the concept of "person," if it is to have argumentative utility, must convey an element of stability. When an act is construed as a function of the person, this continuity will be assumed. Any change will perforce be considered as merely apparent, or possibly as a result of changed circumstances.

Even though the act-person relationship is posited as an immutable feature of reality, the supposed connection of coexistence is really very tenuous. To a certain degree, the phenomena of act and person can be examined separately: "Notions of responsibility, merit, and guilt emphasize the person," whereas "those of norm and rule are primarily preoccupied with the act" ("Act and Person" 254). There is not the same sort of *necessary* link as, say, between an object and its qualities; nonetheless, any separation of the act and the person "is never more than partial and unstable" (254).

The instability in the act-person linkage leads to a constant reciprocal interaction. Kenneth Burke took note of this interaction in *A Grammar of Motives:* "The agent is an author of his acts, which are descended from him, being good progeny if he is good, or bad progeny if he is bad, wise progeny if he is wise, silly progeny if he is silly. And conversely, his acts can make him or remake him in accordance with their nature" (16). Perelman and Olbrechts-Tyteca go further than Burke in stressing this reciprocity. They consider the influence of the act on the person just as striking as that of the person on the act:

> The reaction of the act on the agent is of such a nature as to modify our conception of the person, whether it is a question of new acts which are attributed to him or of former actions which are referred to. Both play an analogous role in argument, although greater weight is given to the more recent acts. Except in limited cases . . . the makeup of the person is never completed, not even by his death. ("Act and Person" 255)

Although persons are free to attempt self-transformations while they live, certain associative techniques enhance the perceived stability of their character traits. Nicknames and epithets are used to manifest such a permanence: Webster was hailed as "godlike Dan'l"; Lincoln, "Honest Abe"; and Nixon, "Tricky Dick." These devices are intended to bring about the adherence of minds by limiting the attention of interlocutors to a single presumed characteristic of the person.

The influence of a person's prestige upon his or her acts was extensively treated in Greek and Roman treatises on rhetoric; and Perelman and Olbrechts-Tyteca give due weight to the classical doctrine of *ethos* in a section entitled "The Speech as an Act of the Speaker" (*The New Rhetoric* 316–321). The proponents of the "new rhetoric" do not break any new theoretical ground in this section or in their treatment of the act-person relationship in general. The most notable feature of their discussion is its eclecticism. From sources as disparate as the *Rhetorica ad Herennium*, Aristotle, Isocrates, and Quintilian among the ancients, with copious illustrative material drawn from Bossuet's and La Bruyère's sermons, Lewis Carroll's children's stories, and British parliamentary debates, to the writings of modern scholars like Charles L. Stevenson and Solomon Asch, Perelman and his co-author provide additional insights into the workings of arguments based on the common idea held by most audiences that a person's acts reveal his or her essential nature.

The act-person connection constitutes a model upon which other liaisons of coexistence are based. For instance, the members of a group are presumed to reflect the characteristics of the group in the same way that an act expresses the person. In a reciprocal way, "membership in a group can, in fact, raise the presumption that certain qualities will be found in its members" (*The New Rhetoric* 322). Argumentation in the human sciences frequently makes use of this line of reasoning, as Perelman explains:

> When the historical sciences shift their focus of interest from individuals to peoples, eras, institutions, and political and economic regimes, they lay stress on new categories, formed in imitation of the person. As the person is manifested through his acts, so also are national groups manifested as entities through their members. Thus one can speak of *Volksgeist*. But on the other hand, besides the idea people have of a group, the favorable or unfavorable preconception they have of it also influences the attitude they adopt toward those who make it up. (*Realm of Rhetoric* 98)

The logical and rhetorical problems posed by the individual-group liaison are markedly more complex, however, than the analogous act-person relationship. For one thing, an individual is usually a member of several groups, and it is not always apparent which one is the most relevant to the case at hand. Presidential candidate John F. Kennedy was able to deflect, if not completely eliminate, the nagging issue of his religion in the 1960 campaign. He did so by confronting the question head-on in a speech to the Greater Houston Ministerial Association. "I am not the Catholic candidate for President," Kennedy told the Protestant preachers. "I am the Democratic party's candidate for President, who happens also to be a Catholic" (Ryan 175). Rather than using a "technique of severance," in Perelman's jargon, to dissociate himself from the Catholic church, Kennedy opted for a "technique of restraint." He placed his religious faith in a broader context and accentuated his role as the designated institutional spokesperson of the Democratic party, a group that was arguably more relevant to the political contest that was underway. Sixteen years later Texas Congresswoman Barbara C. Jordan adopted a different rhetorical strategy when, as an African American woman, she faced the delegates to the 1976 Democratic National Convention as a keynote speaker. She began:

> One hundred and forty-four years ago, members of the Democratic Party first met in convention to select a Presidential candidate. Since that time, Democrats have continued to convene once every four years and draft a party platform and nominate a Presidential candidate. And our meeting this week is a continuation of that tradition.
>
> But there is something different tonight. There is something special about tonight. What is special? I, Barbara Jordan, am a keynote speaker.
>
> A lot of years passed since 1832, and during that time it would have been most unusual for any national political party to ask that a Barbara Jordan

> deliver a keynote address . . . but tonight here I am. And I feel that notwithstanding the past that my presence here is one additional bit of evidence that the American Dream need not forever be deferred. (Ryan 275)

Although Jordan was a member of the U.S. House of Representatives, in that historic moment it was more compelling to highlight her gender and race. As Perelman notes, "A member of a minority group is more easily considered representative than is a member of a majority: a black lost in a white population, a white among blacks, a foreigner among a mass of people native to a region all more readily allow for a generalization to be made from them" (*Realm of Rhetoric* 99). The bond is strongest when that person is a designated spokesperson—an ambassador, party leader, or church official. When the individual-group liaison is weak, the bond is more easily severed by argumentation. Persons born in the U.S. during the post-World War II era are loosely styled "baby boomers." Apart from a few demographic factors—notably age—they have little in common. By adducing counterexamples, exceptions to the rule, and conflicting data, one can easily refute sweeping claims about that generation's cultural preferences or moral behavior.

Because members of a group don't always manifest the typical characteristics of the group, and since not all acts reflect a person's customary behavior, how are exceptions to be accounted for? Very often other relations of coexistence—the relations between *act* and *essence*, for example—are invoked; and various associative techniques are then used to explain away the discrepancy while leaving the interlocutor's conception of reality intact. A person who does not fit in with his or her era will be labeled a precursor or, perhaps, a laggard who has not caught up with the times. A work of art not representative of the author's habitual style will be attributed to outside influences or dismissed as degenerative, not a true expression of the artist's unique genius. "Whatever does not correspond to the image of the essence becomes exceptional," write Perelman and Olbrechts-Tyteca, "and this exception will be justified by one or the other of innumerable possible explanations" (*The New Rhetoric* 327). The concept of essence is remarkably malleable; it allows a speaker or writer to account for a variety of events and actions without the necessity of having to destabilize the structure of reality envisaged by the audience.

As has become evident, the verbal devices based upon sequential and coexistential relations rely upon a vision of reality that can be altered, reinterpreted, or even restructured. Unlike the arguments to be examined in the next chapter, these devices do not "create" reality; they begin with premises already embedded in the worldview of an audience. The plight of the masses during the Depression constituted a "recalcitrance," from which Huey Long could argue that glaring inequities in the distribution of wealth had created the intolerable social injustices of that era. The amassment of British troops in the American colonies backed up Patrick Henry's accusations concerning the malevolent intentions of the British ministry. To see how the same "reality" furnishes a basis for arguments leading to startlingly different conclusions, however, let us look to a period almost a century and a half after Henry spoke to the Virginia assembly.

The occasion was a luncheon of the Clyde Navigation Trustees in Glasgow, Scotland, on February 9, 1912. The speaker was the First Lord of the Admiralty, Winston Churchill, whose thesis was that Great Britain must maintain her dominance of the seas in the face of a growing threat from one of the Continental powers. In his speech Churchill propounded an argument he had made before and would continue to make many times in the decades ahead. Founding his argumentation on a rock-solid geographical fact, the British naval chief drew the following contrast:

> There is . . . this difference between the British naval power and the naval power of the great and friendly Empire—and I trust it may long remain the great and friendly Power—of Germany. The British Navy is to us a necessity and, from some points of view, the German Navy is to them more in the nature of a luxury. Our naval power involves British existence. It is existence to us; it is expansion to them. We cannot menace the peace of a single Continental hamlet, nor do we wish to do so no matter how great and supreme our Navy may become. But, on the other hand, the whole fortunes of our race and Empire, the whole treasure accumulated during so many centuries of sacrifice and achievement would perish and be swept utterly away if our naval supremacy were to be impaired. It is the British Navy which makes Great Britain a Great Power. But Germany was a Great Power, respected and honoured all over the world, before she had a single ship. (Churchill II, 1910)

To the friends of the Royal Navy assembled in Glasgow, the map of Europe itself provided confirmation of Churchill's reasoning. The same map, however, conjured up another version of reality for Germans bottled up in landlocked Berlin. Isolated from warm water seaports and limited in their ability to defend their overseas possessions and extend their empire, they deemed it necessary to build a navy formidable enough to counterbalance the British fleet. Beginning from the same structure of reality, therefore, Churchill concluded that a strong German navy was a luxury, whereas the Germans thought of it as a necessity. Even the most intractable elements of physical or geographic reality become starting points of argumentation only after they have been assimilated rhetorically during the inventional process.

Because the audience's vision of reality is always shaped by verbal devices, Perelman includes *symbolic* liaisons among the liaisons of coexistence (*Realm of Rhetoric* 101). Symbolic relations result in a new, usually heightened, view of reality. Although these relations are thought of as analogical since the symbol and referent belong to different strata of reality, both elements are fused into a mythical or speculative reality in which they both participate. This fusion occurs, for example, when certain persons or events are considered as "figures" of other persons or events. "Between Adam or Isaac or Joseph and Christ, of whom they are a prefigure, there is no sequential connection in a causal sense," as Perelman and Olbrechts-Tyteca note, "but there is an indefinable relation of coexistence, a participation at the level of the divine vision of reality" (*The New Rhetoric* 332).

Whether the liaisons discussed in this chapter are taken to be symbolic or literal in a physical or organic sense, the salient fact is that they are based solidly upon existing notions of the real accepted by both speaker and audience. To be sure, the reality envisaged may be richly textured and multifaceted, but it does not require a radical restructuring of the interlocutor's worldview. In the next chapter we chronicle the development of arguments used in the service of a more ambitious rhetorical agenda.

CHAPTER 6

Arguments That Establish the Structure of Reality

In the last two chapters we have considered two species of arguments that derive their plausibility from resemblances they bear to logical or mathematical forms, or to the fact that their conclusions flow inexorably from a notion of reality that is already embedded in the minds of the audience. These associative techniques, as we noted, correspond loosely—and from a different organizing perspective—to thought processes that have been recognized by logicians and rhetoricians for centuries. Aristotle, for example, identified the syllogism as the basic structure of deduction in his *Analytics*, and in his *Rhetoric* asserted that all persuasive proofs could be reduced to two kinds: "The example is an induction, the enthymeme is a syllogism. . . . I call the enthymeme a rhetorical syllogism, and the example a rhetorical induction. Every one who effects persuasion through proof does in fact use either enthymemes or examples: there is no other way" (1356 b 2–7).

Since arguments based on the structure of reality follow the pattern of logical deduction in Perelman's system, the question naturally arises: How do rhetorical inductions enter into the New Rhetoric? The simplest answer is that these devices function to establish the structure of reality.

This chapter explores the means by which a speaker or writer seeks to bring about an adherence of minds whenever an existing view of reality cannot be invoked as an argumentative starting point. To understand the rhetorical dilemma that gives rise to argumentation designed to fashion a new reality, let us examine an extended line of reasoning put forth by a notable public speaker at a critical juncture in the history of the United States.

The date was February 27, 1860; the place was the Cooper Union Institute in New York City; and the speaker was Abraham Lincoln of Illinois.

The Young Men's Central Republican Union had invited the Westerner to give a public lecture on a theme of his choosing before an audience composed mostly of Republicans who were intently looking forward to that year's presidential election. The speech, as it turned out, became a sort of audition for a possible Lincoln candidacy.

Lincoln had gained notoriety as a result of a series of debates he had participated in during the 1858 Illinois Senate campaign against Stephen A. Douglas. Douglas, who narrowly defeated Lincoln in the vote held in the Illinois legislature, was likely to be the Democratic presidential nominee, and Lincoln viewed the New York address as an opportunity to extend the public dialogue on a leading issue of the day—Douglas's "popular sovereignty" doctrine, which held that Congress lacked the constitutional authority to prohibit slavery in the federal territories. Douglas left open the possibility that territorial residents themselves might choose to restrict slavery, but by asserting that the Constitution withheld from Congress the power to do so, he committed himself to a specific interpretation of what the framers of the document had had in mind. Indeed Douglas had observed in a speech in Ohio just a few months earlier that, "*Our fathers, when they framed the government under which we live, understood this question just as well, and even better, than we do now*" (Lincoln 517). Lincoln seized upon these words as he began his speech, promising to make the Illinois senator's declaration a text for his own address.

No argument based upon the structure of reality could have been advanced on the popular sovereignty question in 1860, for the Constitution had been mute on the subject. No major premise beginning with "The Constitution prohibits [or allows]" could have created the basis of a syllogism supporting either side of the dispute. Whatever conclusion one reached, it would have to be built *inductively*, piece by piece, from the scraps of information available in the public record. This Lincoln proceeded to do.

The Constitution consisted in 1860 of the original document written by the thirty-nine men in 1787, together with twelve amendments, the first ten of which were added in 1789. These were the "fathers" alluded to by Douglas, who presumably "understood the question just as well, and even better, than we do now." Lincoln undertook a painstaking itemization of all the actions—chiefly voting records from subsequent congresses—that shed light on how the framers viewed the question at issue. In Chapter 8 we will notice Lincoln's arrangement and ordering of these historical records as a critical element in the building of his argument. Here let us attend to the *form* of

Lincoln's argument—the manner in which he marshaled a host of particulars to reach a general conclusion.

In 1784, before the Constitution was adopted, only the Northwestern Territory was owned by the United States. The question of whether to prohibit slavery in that territory arose. Four of the thirty-nine were in that legislature. Roger Sherman, Thomas Mifflin, and Hugh Williamson voted for the prohibition; only James McHenry voted against it (without disputing the power of Congress to pass such a law).

Sixteen of the thirty-nine were in the Congress of 1789 when the Ordinance of '87 prohibiting slavery in the Northwest Territory was unanimously passed. Lincoln recited each name.

On and on he went, in lawyerly fashion, adducing evidence from the voting records of the signers of the Constitution, until he reached his destination:

> Here, then, we have twenty-three out of our thirty-nine fathers "who framed the government under which we live," who have, upon their official responsibility and their corporal oaths, acted upon the very question which the text affirms they "understood just as well, and even better, than we do now;" and twenty-one of them—a clear majority of the whole "thirty-nine"—so acting upon it as to make them guilty of gross political impropriety and wilful perjury if, in their understanding, any proper division between local and federal authority, or anything in the Constitution they had made themselves, and sworn to support, forbade the Federal Government to control as to slavery in the federal territories. Thus the twenty-one acted; and, as actions speak louder than words, so actions under such responsibility speak still louder. (Lincoln 522)

Even the two of the twenty-three who voted against prohibition of slavery in the territories, Lincoln went on to say, left no record of their reasons. Hence it could not be assumed that they denied the power of Congress to legislate on the matter.

The extended argument of Lincoln at Cooper Union illustrates the way an edifice of "reality" can be raised, brick by brick, from scattered particulars. In pre-Civil War America, the practice of public opinion polling lay in the distant future; but if the prevailing attitudes of the citizenry had been surveyed, the results would likely have shown that people either had no fixed opinion of whether the Constitution empowered Congress to prohibit slavery in the territories, or else they believed the national legislature had no such authority. In either case, Lincoln's rhetorical task was to establish for his hearers and readers the structure of a *new* outlook on the issue at hand.

When discrete elements are linked together, the plausibility inherent in their liaisons invests the thesis to which they are connected with an added credibility. Perelman and Olbrechts-Tyteca distinguish two associative devices that can be utilized to restructure an audience's view of the real: (1) resorting to a specific case, which is presented as an *exemplum* of a particular relation in reality; and (2) suggesting a correspondence between facts or circumstances already acknowledged by the audience and a relation or structure the speaker wants the audience to accept. The persuader, in other words, can either bring forward a case in point or draw an analogy.

Argumentation by Example, Illustration, and Model

The structure of reality can be established, first of all, by resorting to the particular case. This form of argument takes three forms: "as an example, it makes generalization possible; as an illustration, it provides support for an already established regularity; as a model, it encourages imitation" (*The New Rhetoric* 350). While the Belgian authors' treatment of these devices in their major treatise is not particularly striking or unique, we can see from their discussion how the notion of rhetorical reason plays out in actual argumentation. Perelman's Rule of Justice, which dictates equal treatment for beings of the same essential category, provides the "logical" basis for taking a specific case as a starting point for a generalization about reality. In effect, the speaker, by subordinating the individual case to a generalization, "introduces his [or her] audience to a rule about reality" (van Eemeren *et al.* 240).

To see how examples may be used to transform an existing view of reality, let us posit, merely for purposes of illustration, a prevailing public assumption—namely, that the presidency of the United States is a safe occupation. People are generally aware of the extensive precautions taken by the Secret Service and other security offices to ensure the protection of the president. Assume that a speaker wishes to convince an audience that *the presidency is really a very dangerous office to hold.* In order to support that generalization, one might set forth an example: *President Lincoln was assassinated in 1865*. If interlocutors acknowledge the factuality of this example and grasp the warrant connecting it to the thesis being advocated, they perceive the principle of inductive reasoning—whether or not they label it as such—upon which the argument rests. They might, however, resist the claim if it is supported by only one example; perhaps the Lincoln assassination was an isolated aberration. Sensing the need for more proof, the arguer adduces more examples:

President Garfield was mortally wounded in 1881.
President McKinley was killed in 1901.
President Kennedy was assassinated in 1963.

By now, the thesis has taken on added weight. Perhaps the auditors have begun to revise their assumptions about the president's security. If additional instances are deemed necessary, the speaker might point to the severe wounding of Ronald Reagan, the shooting of Theodore Roosevelt, and the near misses of shots fired at Franklin D. Roosevelt, Gerald Ford, and so on. At some point, even the most recalcitrant listener will be likely to concede the truth behind the speaker's thesis.

How does the adduction of specific instances lead to a changed worldview? The answer carries us beyond our present focus on logical and rhetorical processes into the realm of social psychology. Although Perelman did not seek confirmation for his philosophical ideas about induction in the findings of social scientists, it is nonetheless instructive to note the observations of Dolf Zillmann and Hans-Bernd Brosius, who have recently conducted extensive investigations into the influence of case studies on the perception of issues. In the preface to their book, *Exemplification in Communication*, these authors state:

> Exemplification is fundamental to the perception of the so-called real world. As segments of pertinent experience that are stored in memory, exemplars provide samplings of information about past occurrences that foster dispositions and ultimately direct behavior toward similar occurrences on later encounter. A limited number of experiences thus serve as the basis for judging a larger body of similar occurrences. The implicit generalization amounts to a spontaneously executed inductive inference. Inferences of this kind are made by all species capable of adaptation through learning. Humans, no doubt, have made these influences through the millennia, and they are still making them, routinely so and nonconsciously for the most part. (vii)

In the case of inductive reasoning, logic and psychologic converge to buttress Perelman's claim about the centrality of the Rule of Justice in the functioning of rationality in its broadest sense.

It should be underscored, however, that the rationality underlying inductive inferences manifests itself only when an audience accords the individual cases that serve as examples the status of facts. If they are challenged, the generalization is jeopardized, as van Eemeren and his colleagues rightly point out. The Dutch authors then add nuances to Perelman and Olbrechts-Tyteca's discussion of argumentation by example:

> Discussion about the status of the cases that are to serve as the starting point for the generalization can, incidentally, be quite useful if the speaker can easily demonstrate their factual nature, because this distracts attention from the manner in which the generalization is made ("Don't you believe Tiddles is deaf? Just clap your hands and you'll see; that's precisely what I'm trying to get into your head: white cats are always deaf"). If the audience is convinced that the example given is indeed to be regarded as a fact, this can add to the ease with which the generalization is accepted.

Nor is it possible to predict with precision the number of examples needed to establish or destroy a rule:

> In contrast to formal language, in colloquial language it is certainly not often possible to refute the existence of a rule (i.e. *falsify* it) by means of only one counter-example. The ambiguity of language provides too many escape routes, and it is also possible to take refuge in an *exception*. (van Eemeren *et al.* 241)

To be sure, a single, well-chosen exception can sometimes demolish a generalization; yet it is also true that one example often suffices to drive a point home.

Instead of trying to fabricate a general rule, an argument can proceed *from one particular case to another*. Aristotle provided a specimen of this sort of reasoning, which Perelman and Olbrechts-Tyteca cited in *The New Rhetoric* in a discursive form. When Perelman appropriated the same example for *The Realm of Rhetoric*, he reduced it to its essence: "As the Persian kings Darius and Xerxes did not cross the Aegean until after seizing Egypt, the present Persian king will also cross over into Europe if he seizes Egypt" (107; see also *The New Rhetoric* 352; *Rhetoric* 1393 b 31–35). In a similar vein, President Richard Nixon sought to justify his decision to order U.S. military forces to attack North Vietnamese bases in Cambodia, when he argued in a nationally broadcast speech on May 15, 1970, that "to desert 18 million South Vietnamese people who have put their trust in us [would] expose them to the same slaughter and savagery which the leaders of North Vietnam inflicted on hundreds of thousands of North Vietnamese who chose freedom when the Communists took over North Vietnam in 1954" (Ryan 167). As with all arguments in which a particular case is invoked, whether it is as the basis for a generalization or as the counterpart of a parallel case, the success of Nixon's claim hinged upon the incontestability of his assumption about the "atrocities" of 1954. For most Americans in 1970, the factuality of this assumption was not likely to be disputed.

Both the Rule of Justice and the principle of *inertia* come into play whenever examples are used in argumentation. It seems natural "to subsume under the same rule situations that have been described in the same way," and "it is the desire to differentiate situations described by the same term that needs justification" (*Realm of Rhetoric* 108). In "juridical logic," as we saw in Chapter 3, precedents play a primary role; in effect, they establish a legal presumption or "judicial reality," against which inertia an opposing jurist is forced to offer counterarguments in support of an alternative reality.

The particular case plays a different role whenever it is used not to establish a general rule, but to illustrate a rule that has already been established. The function of an illustration is to strengthen the audience's adherence to a previously accepted, though perhaps tentatively held, notion of reality. It serves to clarify a general statement, show its import by pointing out its various applications, and, most importantly, "increase its presence to the consciousness." Unlike an example, an illustration does not have to be beyond dispute; the rule it illustrates does not depend on it. The main thing is that "it should strike the imagination forcibly so as to win attention" (*The New Rhetoric* 357). Thus, Aristotle illustrates the inferiority of the loose ("free-running") style of composition as compared to the more vigorous periodic structure. "Every one used this method formerly;" he writes, "not many do so now":

> By "free-running" style I mean the kind that has no natural stopping places, and comes to a stop only because there is no more to say of that subject. This style is unsatisfying just because it goes on indefinitely—one always likes to sight a stopping-place in front of one: it is only at the goal that men in a race faint and collapse; while they see the end of the course before them, they can keep going. (*Rhetoric* 1409 a 27–34)

"The transition from example to illustration occurs almost imperceptibly in cases in which a rule is justified before being illustrated," says Perelman. "The first examples need to be generally accepted, since their role is to give the rule credibility; the others, once the rule is accepted, will in turn be supported by it" (*Realm of Rhetoric* 108). In Lincoln's lengthy recitation of the public actions and voting records of the thirty-nine founding fathers in his Cooper Union speech, the first series of specific cases functioned as examples to support the idea that the framers did not intend to prohibit Congress from controlling the spread of slavery in the federal territories. At some point in Lincoln's argumentation, as the audience came to concede the truth of his thesis, the particular instances took on the character of illustrations, reinforcing the principle that had been established.

Sometimes the specific case is used in argument neither to establish nor to illustrate a general rule, but to set before the audience a model to be imitated. By doing so, the speaker takes advantage of the prestige accorded to a respected model in the hope that listeners will be led to imitate the behavior of the model. F. H. van Eemeren and his co-authors write: "The model may consist of a historical figure or being represented as perfect" (242). The apostle Paul had both types in mind when he wrote to the Corinthians, "Be ye followers [imitators] of me, even as I also am of Christ" (*I Cor.* 11:1). And to the Thessalonians he expressed his joy that they had already adopted the model, adding, "So that ye were ensamples to all that believe in Macedonia and Achaia" (*I Thess.* 1:7). Argumentation by model is intrinsically appealing to speakers and writers, for it enables them to highlight relevant aspects of the model—even when it is unique or ideal—and draw a suitable application from it.

If the model is too eminent or renowned, the argument can backfire. Holding up the great Nobel prize-winning missionary and doctor Albert Schweitzer to us in order to provoke us to perform heroic sacrifices for humanity could have the opposite effect of discouraging us from such exertions. "If on the other hand our neighbour Nilsen takes off for Africa one day and founds a little hospital there," writes Arne Naess, "that might be more likely to get us moving" (qtd in van Eemeren *et al.* 242). And we have the instructive example of the father telling his son who was lagging in his studies, "At your age, Napoleon was top of his class," to which his son replied, "At your age, he was emperor" (*The New Rhetoric* 368). This example shows that models held up for imitation need to be heedfully chosen, or else when they are used to tip the scales of reality in one direction, counterexamples or *antimodels* can quickly redress the balance in the other. Moreover, whether a specific case is presented to us as a being or object that we should try to resemble, or avoid at all costs, depends upon the perspectives of the arguer and presumed audience. Depending on one's ideological predilection, for instance, a socialist utopia can be considered a model or an antimodel.

We began this chapter by showing how Abraham Lincoln assembled, from the available bits of historical data, a plausible interpretation of how the authors of the Constitution understood a critical aspect of the slavery question.

Lincoln's method involved the meticulous accumulation of specific cases, and the thesis that resulted became a tenet of Republican orthodoxy. The rhetorical posture adopted by the Illinoisan was instrumental in winning for him that party's nomination as a presidential candidate in 1860. To see how the resort to the particular case played a consequential part in another fateful episode in U.S. history, let us shift our attention to an event that took place almost a century later half a world beyond American shores.

A meeting occurred on August 23, 1950, in a sixth floor conference room in the *Dai Ichi* Building in Tokyo, Japan. The occasion was a strategic planning session convened to determine the most effective military response to an invasion of South Korea by the North Korean People's Army. The onslaught began on June 25 and, by late August, the invaders had overrun the capital city of Seoul and threatened to drive the remaining American forces entirely from the Korean peninsula. Present were General Douglas MacArthur, UN Supreme Commander for Korea; several members of his Far East Headquarters staff; and two members of the Joint Chiefs of Staff, General Lawton Collins (Army Chief of Staff) and Admiral Forrest Sherman. The purpose of Collins's and Sherman's trip to Japan, MacArthur believed, was to dissuade him from pursuing the course of action he had already decided upon—an audacious and highly risky landing of UN forces at Inchon on Korea's west coast. The amphibious landing would be 150 miles behind the North Korean lines, 25 miles from Seoul, and, if successful, would liberate the capital, cut the enemy's supply lines, and jeopardize the North Korean capital, Pyongyang.

The case against the Inchon landing was presented in a methodical fashion by Rear Admiral James H. Doyle, the Navy's Far East expert on amphibious techniques. Doyle brought eight staff members into the small conference room, one by one, each presenting a bleak account of the physical and logistical obstacles that would have to be overcome at Inchon. Then MacArthur, whose "end run" strategy for enveloping the Japanese forces had succeeded brilliantly a few years earlier in the Southwest Pacific, took the floor. No transcript exists of his 45-minute speech, but the few who heard it have called it a "soliloquy which no one present would ever forget," a "Churchillian oration," and "oratory such as the world seldom sees save from the orchestra seats of a theatre" (qtd in Carpenter 4). Rhetorical scholar Ronald H. Carpenter has reconstructed from extant records, including MacArthur's own *Reminiscences*, the arguments employed by opponents of the Inchon strategy, as well as the reasoning of the General himself. All of the surviving accounts agree that while MacArthur acknowledged the formidable hazards connected to his daring stratagem—reckoning the odds against it at 5,000 to one, by one estimation—he nevertheless expressed confidence that the Navy would surmount the barriers associated with the tides and the terrain. "We shall land at Inchon and I shall crush them," several sources quote him as saying.

The centerpiece of MacArthur's argumentation was the element of surprise. Even though speculation concerning a landing at Inchon was rampant among American soldiers and reporters, who dubbed it "Operation Common Knowledge" at the Tokyo Press Club, MacArthur thought the North Koreans would never believe such an attack would occur. To bolster his case, he reached back to the French and Indian War for an historical parallel:

> As an example, the Marquis de Montcalm believed in 1759 that it was impossible for an armed force to scale the precipitous river banks south of the then walled city of Quebec, and therefore concentrated his formidable defenses along the more vulnerable banks north of the city. But General James Wolfe and a small force did indeed come up the St. Lawrence River and scale those heights. On the Plains of Abraham, Wolfe won a stunning victory that was made possible almost entirely by surprise. Thus he captured Quebec and in effect ended the French and Indian War. Like Montcalm, the North Koreans would regard an Inchon landing as impossible. Like Wolfe, I could take them by surprise. (Carpenter 5)

According to Carpenter, this one example was the *only* element of support for any assertion made during MacArthur's lengthy exposition. In effect, the model of Wolfe's victory at Quebec—and the absence of any competing antimodel—was the crucial element, as Carpenter concludes, "conducing to MacArthur's success in oratory altering the course of history" (11).

From the particulars of human knowledge and experience, whether from history or science or even the realms of myth and creative imagination, practitioners of argument spin out altered world views. Examples, illustrations, and models for emulation, if well chosen, can bring about an entirely new way of looking at things. Another technique for establishing the structure of reality involves the juxtaposition of a well-known entity from one sphere with a lesser-known entity from another sphere in such a way as to illuminate both entities. To this final class of associative devices we now turn.

Argumentation by Analogy

Perelman and Olbrechts-Tyteca hold that analogical reasoning plays a primary role in argumentation of all kinds, from disagreements around the family dinner table to the most recondite disputations among scientists or philosophers. The Belgian authors disagree with the formal and mathematical logicians who deny that analogy has any power to convince, "when the mere fact that it can make us prefer one hypothesis to another shows that it has argumentative value" (*The New Rhetoric* 372). "The argumentative value of analogy," they write, "can be most clearly seen if it is envisaged as a resemblance of structures, the most general formulation of which is: *A* is to *B* as C is to *D*. This conception of analogy is in line with a very ancient tradition, still followed by Kant, Whately, and Cournot" (372). Recourse to analogy is frequently at the center of an original conception of the universe, whether it appears in metaphysical thought or in a scientific paradigm.

The distinction between Perelman's "rhetorical reason" and the rationality envisaged by the mathematical logicians can be perceived clearly in *The Realm of Rhetoric*, where Perelman acknowledges *proportion* to be the essence of analogy, but adds an important caveat:

> [Analogy] differs from the purely mathematical proportion insofar as it does not posit the *equality* of two relations but rather affirms a *similitude* between them. Whereas in algebra positing $a/b = c/d$ makes it possible to affirm $c/d = a/b$ symmetrically and to bring out, on these terms, mathematical operations which result in equations (e.g., $ad—cb = 0$), in analogy we affirm that *a* is to *b* as *c* is to *d*. It is no longer a question of division but of the comparison of some relationship to another. (114–115)

In Perelman's view, a new insight into reality is obtained as a consequence of the interaction between the pairs of terms in an analogy. To illustrate its inner workings as an associative device, Perelman and Olbrechts-Tyteca offer a "typical analogy" from Aristotle's *Metaphysics:*

> "For as the eyes of bats are to the blaze of day, so is the reason in our soul to the things which are by nature most evident of all." A and *B* together, the terms to which the conclusion relates (reason in the soul, obviousness) we call the *theme*, and C and *D* together, the terms that serve to buttress the argument (eyes of bats, blaze of day), we shall call the *phoros*. In the ordinary course, the phoros is better known than the theme of which it should clarify the structure or establish the value, either its value as a whole or the respective value of its components. (*The New Rhetoric* 373)

The distinctions between theme and phoros are strikingly reminiscent of I. A. Richards's contrasts between the *tenor* and *vehicle* in metaphor in *The Philosophy of Rhetoric* (96–101). Numerous references to Richards's works in *The New Rhetoric* indicate that the British literary critic and semanticist influenced the Belgian writers in their exploration of the relationship between style and argument (chiefly, one suspects, through Lucie Olbrechts-Tyteca). In Chapter 9 we shall consider at greater length Perelman's concept of metaphor, which he and his co-author defined as "a condensed analogy, resulting from the fusion of an element from the phoros with an element from the theme" (402). Here it is sufficient to note that analogy brings together two pairs of previously unconnected elements from disparate domains to create, strengthen, or intensify the adherence of minds to a persuasive thesis.

The insistence that theme and phoros must be from different spheres is at the core of Perelman's definition of analogy: "When the two relations encountered belong to the same sphere, and can be subsumed under a common structure, we have not analogy but argument by example or illustration" (373). For this reason, MacArthur's invocation of Wolfe's attack upon Quebec as an argument for his proposed landing at Inchon can be termed a model (or example for emulation) rather than an analogy, since both elements of the comparison are drawn from military strategy. What others have called the "literal analogy" is rendered meaningless in Perelman's scheme (Measell 67). On the other hand, Lincoln, unlike MacArthur, was certainly reasoning by analogy—actually in its compressed, metaphorical form—when he wrote to General Joseph Hooker on June 14, 1863: "If the head of Lee's army is at Martinsburg, and the tail of it on the Plank road between Fredericksburg & Chancellorsville, the animal must be very slim somewhere. Could you not break him?" (Lincoln 708–709) Comparing an army to a beast enabled Lincoln to bring out shared salient qualities—elongation and vulnerability—that pointed to a promising battle maneuver.

In addition to the fact that the theme and phoros belong to different realms, "What distinguishes analogy fundamentally from simple mathematical proportion is that in analogy the nature of the terms of the theme is never a matter of indifference" (*The New Rhetoric* 373). The value of the terms of the theme is either enhanced or depreciated as a result of the interaction that occurs when A and C and *B* and *D* are brought closer together. To illustrate a negative transfer of value from theme to phoros, Perelman and Olbrechts-Tyteca draw upon an analogy used by John Calvin:

> "The election of Amadeus (Duke of Savoy), duly solemnized by the authority of a general and holy council, went up in smoke, except that the aforesaid Amadeus was appeased by a cardinal's hat, as a barking dog by a morsel." The devaluation of the terms of the theme [Amadeus : cardinal's hat] is brought about by the choice of terms for the phoros [barking dog : morsel];

> but the value attached to these terms is itself derived, in part at least, from their use in the analogy. The attitude of a barking dog is not one that necessarily calls for a depreciatory judgment. (378)

In what sense, one might ask, are the terms of this analogy brought closer through the interaction of theme and phoros? Although Perelman does not address this question expressly, "The implication here is that the terms are seen to be subsumed under the same general law," as James Measell has pointed out. "One must realize that the general law ('rewards influence behavior' in the analogy above) is neither stated explicitly in the analogy nor even apparent to the audience until both theme and phoros have been fully articulated by the speaker" (68–69). In effect, with the phoros as a starting point, the analogy restructures the reality associated with the theme by giving it a conceptual setting in which the importance of a cardinal's hat is devalued.

Analogies are important but precarious techniques of argument. Interlocutors who reject the conclusion will tend to dismiss the posited relationship as merely a vague resemblance, while insisting that "there is not even an analogy." In contrast, the person who invokes an analogy will almost always claim "it is more than just a simple analogy." The result is that the analogy is "stuck between two disavowals—disavowal by its opponents and disavowal by its supporters" (*The New Rhetoric* 393). Moreover, the distinction between spheres cannot always be made to the satisfaction of an audience: "It is only in certain analogies of recognized type, such as allegories and fables, that the distinction between the two spheres appears beyond argument" (393).

Analogies can be an argumentative instrument of overwhelming power. In a speech to unionized sanitation workers in Memphis, Tennessee, on the night of April 3, 1968, Martin Luther King, Jr., employed the imagery of the Biblical Exodus to suggest that the Israelites' march from captivity was similar to the labor dispute in which his listeners were currently engaged. In his stirring peroration, King donned the mantle of Moses as he spoke of his own role in the larger civil rights movement, of which the Memphis strike was a part:

> Well, I don't know what will happen now. We've got some difficult days ahead. But it really doesn't matter with me now. Because I've been to the mountaintop. And I don't mind. Like anybody, I would like to live a long life. Longevity has its place. But I'm not concerned about that now. I just

> want to do God's will. And he's allowed me to go up to the mountain. And I've looked over. And I've seen the promised land. I may not get there with you. But I want you to know tonight. I'm not worried about anything. I'm not fearing any man. Mine eyes have seen the glory of the coming of the Lord. (King 205)

After a lengthy analysis of King's use of narrative as an inventional strategy, Thomas Rosteck concludes that the illustrative story of the Exodus, in which the civil rights leader invited a comparison between himself and Moses, functioned "as both a metaphor and as an example." Influenced by Ricoeur's idea that "one and the same strategy of discourse puts into play the logical force of analogy and the power to set things before the eyes, ultimately the capacity to signify active reality," Rosteck writes: "It is this power of discourse to 'make' experience 'mean' that offered to the audience of King's 'I've Been to the Mountaintop' oration, an urgency and a sense of their own destiny" (Rosteck 31). Whether, in the final analysis, Dr. King's eerily prescient narrative is best defined as a resort to a particular case (illustration) or as an extended analogy, it cannot be gainsaid that the audience in Memphis—and later audiences touched by the address—came to view the struggle for equal rights for African Americans in a new light. Although the Exodus story had been invoked by King and others before that night, the image of the martyred civil rights leader as Moses became indelibly stamped in the public consciousness after his death the next day. A restructuring of the social reality perceived by millions of Americans had occurred, creating a transfiguration in both the image of King and in the movement of which he was a part.

Argumentation based upon analogical relations, therefore, like reasoning from particular cases, is a means for establishing a view of the real in the minds of an audience. Both modes of rationality, like quasi-logical arguments and arguments based on the structure of reality, facilitate the association of ideas. All of these devices serve to connect and make interdependent elements that could otherwise be considered independent. This is not to say that refutation cannot succeed in severing the links or destroying the grounds for connecting these associations in the first place. For example, an analogy can be flatly rejected. Auditors may refuse to accept any similarity between the modern civil rights movement and the wanderings of the ancient Israelites. In such a case, opponents will affirm "that elements which should remain separate and independent have been improperly associated" (*The New Rhetoric* 411).

But there is another process in argumentation that is capable of altering an audience's view of reality in more profound ways. Instead of merely severing linkages, the process to which we next turn involves a radical modification of the elements that comprise the conceptual data of arguments, resulting in a restructuring of the elements themselves.

CHAPTER 7

Rhetoric as a Technique and a Mode of Truth

Henry Johnstone and Chaim Perelman were friends, but their friendship did not prevent Johnstone from criticizing Perelman's work, sometimes severely. Central to Johnstone's concerns was an issue that has dogged rhetoric since its beginnings in ancient Greece: Is it a technique, or is it a mode of truth? In one of his many criticisms of *The New Rhetoric*, Johnstone complains about its chapter, "The Dissociation of Concepts," that "one is never sure whether [Perelman is] thinking of rhetoric primarily as a technique or primarily as a mode of truth. One wonders, too, what status [he is] claiming for the book itself" (99).[1] Since the chapter in question largely concerns philosophical argument, the doubt is very much à propos. But the response to Johnstone's implied question—a response that Johnstone does not think available—is that the correct answer legitimately varies in a systematic way. While in philosophical contexts, and, incidentally, in scientific ones, rhetoric is invariably a mode of truth, in contexts of public address it need not be. To see how this systematic variation might be the case, we will focus, as does Johnstone, on the dissociation of concepts as a test case of the robustness of a rhetoric oriented toward truth. For Perelman and his co-author, Lucie Olbrechts-Tyteca, all dissociations of concepts are rhetorical strategies. But they are not all equal. To explore these differences, we must first define dissociation, and then come to terms with the way in which concepts are dissociated in public address, in philosophy, and in science. In treating these examples, we intend to illustrate the wide scope of Perelman and Olbrechts-Tyteca's ideas; in doing so, however, we must be wary. While dissociations will vary systematically according to field, they are not each instances of any general "law." Johnstone is surely right to "doubt whether there is any general logic of dissociation; there is only the logic of each particular dissociation, generated in each case by a particular problem" (99). When we have run through our illustrations, we can return to Johnstone's question about the status of rhetoric and of Perelman's study of it.

Dissociation vs. Breaking the Links

In the midst of the Civil War, in a letter to his good friend, James C. Conkling, a letter meant to be read publicly at a meeting of Union supporters that Lincoln could not attend, the President tackles the issue of the cause for which the War is being fought:

> You say you will not fight to free negroes. Some of them seem willing to fight for you; but, no matter. Fight you, then, exclusively to save the Union. I issued the [Emancipation P]roclamation on purpose to aid you in saving the Union. Whenever you shall have conquered all resistance to the Union, if I shall urge you to continue fighting, it will be an apt time then, for you to declare that you will not fight to free negroes. (722–723)

In this passage, Lincoln is breaking the links between the fighting of the Civil War and the freeing of the slaves; he is saying, in Perelman and Olbrechts-Tyteca's terms, that he is "affirming that elements that should remain separate and independent have been improperly associated" (411). This is very different from the associated and more important concept of dissociation:

> Dissociation . . . assumes the original unity of elements comprised within a single conception and designated by a single notion. The dissociation of notions brings about a more or less profound change in the conceptual data that are used as the basis of argument. It is then no more a question of breaking the links that join independent elements, but of modifying the very structure of these elements. (411–412)

In the following passage, Lincoln dissociates the founding and flourishing of America from the framing of the Constitution; he does so in the interest of promoting what he sees as the real principle animating our Union and our continuing prosperity, then as now—the principle of liberty to all:

> Without the *Constitution* and the *Union*, we could not have attained the result; but even these, are not the primary cause of our great prosperity. There is something back of these, entwining itself more closely about the human heart. That something, is the principle of "Liberty to all"—the principle that clears the *path* for all—gives *hope* to all—and, by consequence, *enterprize* and *industry* to all.
>
> The *expression* of that principle, in our Declaration of Independence, was most happy, and fortunate. *Without* this, as well as *with* it, we could have declared our independence of Great Britain; but *without* it, we could not, I think, have secured our free government, and consequent prosperity. No oppressed people will *fight* and *endure*, as our fathers did, without the promise of something better, than a mere change of masters. (513)

In forming this dissociation, Lincoln's is "prompted by the desire to remove an incompatibility arising out of the confrontation of one proposition with others" (*NR*, 413). The dissociation assumes an original unity of elements, the notion of a nation whose prosperity has as its cause its Constitution and the Union that Constitution creates. Lincoln feels that this view, because it leads to an incompatibility, is deeply mistaken: No one risks life and limb for a document. The removal of this incompatibility forces us, he thinks, to modify our view: The Constitution and the Union become the means by which the real cause of our continuing prosperity—the principle of liberty to all—works its magic.

Issues are not *a priori* candidates for one treatment or another, breaking the links or dissociation. "Depending on whether connecting links between elements are regarded as 'natural' or 'artificial', as 'essential' or 'accidental'," the Belgians assert, "one person will see a dissociation where another sees only the breaking of a connecting link" (412). This is exactly the case when we compare Lincoln and Douglas on the extension of slavery to the Territories. Douglas stoutly defends the possibility of extension as a right of the states; he feels that the issue has been improperly linked to federal powers—a link that ought to be broken:

> This government was made on the great basis of the sovereignty of the States—the right of each state to regulate its own domestic institutions to suit itself, and that right was conferred with the understanding and expectation that inasmuch as each locality had separate and distinct interests, each state must have different and distinct local and domestic institutions, corresponding to the wants and interests of each locality. Our fathers knew when they made this government that the laws and institutions which were well adapted to the Green Mountains of Vermont were unsuited to the rice plantations of South Carolina. They knew then, as well as we know now, that

> the laws and institutions which would be adapted to the beautiful prairies of Illinois would not be suited to the mining regions of California. They knew that in a Republic as broad as this, having such a variety of soil, of climate and of interests, there must necessarily be a corresponding variety in the local laws, and policy, and institutions of each State, adapted to its own wants and condition. For these reasons this Union was established on the right of each State to do as it pleased on the subject of slavery, and every other question, negativing the right of every other State to complain, much less interfere with such policy. (Lincoln-Douglas 327)

In his response, Lincoln agrees with Douglas about most of these matters, but not on the issue of slavery, which he dissociates from the rest, prompted by the incompatibility he sees between the possible extension of slavery and continuing national peace:

> I ask if there is any parallel between these things and the institution of slavery amongst us? I ask if there is any parallel at all between these things? I ask you to consider well if we have any difficulty or quarrel among ourselves about the cranberry laws of Indiana, or the oyster laws of Virginia, or about the timber laws of Maine and New Hampshire, or about the fact that Louisiana produces sugar and we produce flour and not sugar. When have we had quarrels about these things? Never no such thing. On the other hand, when have we had perfect peace in regard to this thing, which I say is an element of discord in the nation? We have sometimes had peace, and when was that? We have had peace whenever the institution of slavery remained quiet where it was, and we have had turmoil and difficulty whenever it has made a struggle to spread out where it was not. I ask, then, if experience does not teach, if it does not speak in thunder tones, that that policy gives peace being returned to, gives promise of peace again. (Lincoln-Douglas 354)

Having defined dissociation, we will now explore its uses in public address, science, and philosophy.

Dissociation and Public Address

In public address, such dissociations can be merely manipulative, a way of concealing truth by deliberately misinforming, misleading, or withholding information from audiences. We can most easily illustrate this use by referring to the scene in Shakespeare's *Julius Caesar* in which Mark Antony gives the eulogy at the funeral of the just-assassinated Caesar. The speech of the first speaker at the funeral, Brutus, the chief conspirator, is a great success, the audience expressing views that match those of the conspirators:

4 PLEBIAN What does [Antony] say of Brutus?
3 PLEBIAN He says for Brutus' sake
He finds himself beholding to us all.
4 PLEBIAN 'Twere best he speak no harm of Brutus here!
1 PLEBIAN This Caesar was a tyrant.
3 PLEBIAN Nay, that's certain:
We are blest that Rome is rid of him. (3.1.58–63)

Clearly, Antony has his task set out for him. He sees an incompatibility between the view of the conspirators and his own view. In order to inflame the Roman mob against the conspirators, he must show that the real character of his friend was such that the conspirators were murderers, rather than assassins, criminals rather than patriots. Moreover, he must conceal from his audience the fact that he is doing so. Thus he accomplishes his dissociation by means of irony, by seeming to comply with the wishes of the conspirators while, at the same time, undermining the audience's faith in their judgment:

Friends, Romans, countrymen, lend me your ears!
I come to bury Caesar, not to praise him.
The evil that men do lives after them,
The good is oft interrèd in their bones:
So let it be with Caesar. The noble Brutus
Hath told you Caesar was ambitious;
If it were so, it were a grievous fault,
And grievously hath Caesar answered it.
Here under leave of Brutus and the rest—
For Brutus is an honourable man,
So are they all, all honourable men—
Come I to speak at Caesar's funeral. (3.2.65–76)

In this exordium, Antony asserts his intention to give a funeral eulogy that, paradoxically, eschews praise for the deceased. To understand the significance of this paradox, we must adopt two perspectives, that of the Roman mob and that of an audience member or reader. For the mob, this disparagement is in accord with Brutus's wishes; for us it is the beginning of a dissociation between assassination and murder. Take, for example, the parenthesis, "for Brutus is an honourable man, / So are they all, all honourable men," a series of clauses linked neither syntactically nor semantically to the sentence in which they are embedded. For the mob, this series reveals the effort Antony is making to defer to the wishes of the conspirators; for us, its lack of syntactic and semantic connections with the rest of the sentence, coupled with the "unnecessary" repetitions of "honourable," signals the start of a pattern that will eventually reverse the meaning of that crucial adjective, that will make the actions of Brutus all the more criminal to the mob *because* of his noble birth and honorable pretensions:

> O masters, if I were disposed to stir
> Your hearts and minds to mutiny and rage,
> I should do Brutus wrong and Cassius wrong,
> Who (you all know) are honourable men.
> I will not do them wrong; I rather choose
> To wrong the dead, to wrong myself and you,
> Than I will wrong such honourable men. (3.2.113–119)

To the Roman mob, Antony's audience in the play, there is no device in the speech, no irony. For them, Antony is innocently pointing out some obvious facts about his dead friend, facts that in the aggregate challenge the judgment of the conspirators. To us this is irony, a device; to the mob it is merely plain speaking. If the mob were to perceive what we perceive, they would reject Antony's claims: "Everything that promotes perception of a device," Perelman and Olbrechts-Tyteca assert, "will prompt the search for a reality dissociated with it" (453). The reality is that Antony is contemptuous of the mob, is merely using them.[2]

But while dissociation in political rhetoric can be manipulative, it need not be; it can also be a mode by which the speaker shares with his audience the truth as he sees it. Our examples of this positive use come from two speeches of Lincoln: the reply to Douglas in the seventh debate at Alton, Illinois, on October 15, 1858; and the Cooper Institute Address of February 27, 1860. At Alton, in his reply to Douglas, Lincoln probes beneath the surface of his opponent's doctrine of popular sovereignty, a policy according to which the territories have the right to vote slavery up or down, and the Federal government has no right to interfere. Douglas professes to be unconcerned about which way the vote goes. This does not express Douglas's indifference to slavery; rather, it expresses his support for the westward expansion of the United States, an expansion that Douglas feels the vexed issue of Federal jurisdiction over slavery in the Territories will continue to undermine. But Lincoln sees an incompatibility between these views and the central tenet behind the formation of the Union: liberty to all. He therefore insists that the issue only appears to be political; it is really moral. For Lincoln, skepticism about Douglas's motives is merely a means of revealing the tawdriness of his views:

> [Douglas] says he don't care whether [slavery] is voted up or down. Now, I don't care whether that is intended to be expressive of his individual sentiment upon that subject or whether it is intended to be expressive of the national policy that he desires should be carried out; it is alike valuable for my purposes. I can say that a man can logically say that if he sees no wrong in it, but he cannot say so logically if he admits that slavery is wrong. No man can say that he does not care if a wrong is voted up or down, he cannot say he is indifferent as to a wrong; but he must have a choice between right or wrong. He says that whatever community desires slavery has a right to it. He can say so logically if it is not a wrong, but if he admits that it is wrong, he cannot logically say that anybody has a right to do wrong. He says upon the score of equality, slaves should be allowed to go into the territories the same as other property. His argument is logical if the properties are alike, but if one is wrong and the other right, then he cannot say that, for there is no equality between the right and the wrong. I say that everything in the Democratic policy, in the shape it takes in legislation, in the Dred Scott decision, in their conversations, everyone carefully excludes the thought that there is anything wrong in it whatever.
>
> That is the real issue! An issue that will continue in this country when these poor tongues of Douglas and myself shall be silent. These are the two principles that are made the eternal struggle between right and wrong. They are the two principles that have stood face to face . . . , one of them asserting the divine right of kings, the same principle that says you work, you toil, you earn bread, and I will eat it. (Lincoln-Douglas 358–359)

As Zarefsky points out, this degree of eloquence is not typical of the Lincoln-Douglas debates (179–180). It is an eloquence that is distilled into the final antithesis, a contrast between pronouns. The moral issue of slavery could not be more dramatically presented than by a dissociation that equates "our peculiar institution," not with procedural rights guaranteed by the Constitution, but simply with the exploitation of one human being solely for the profit of another.

In the Cooper Institute Address, Lincoln adds to the forcefulness of his case against slavery by engaging in a series of powerful dissociations that shifts perspective gradually but inexorably from the political to the moral; Zarefsky makes the excellent point that the historical argument functions as a surrogate for the moral argument (226). Lincoln's dissociation is impelled as before by the incompatibility between slavery and liberty to all. In this case Lincoln's dissociative device is his reconstruction of the past, a reconstruction he uses to determine the *real* intent of the founders on the issue of the expansion of slavery to the Territories and thereby to undermine *any* political arguments the South chooses to make:

> The sum of the whole is, that of our thirty-nine fathers who framed the original Constitution, twenty-one—a clear majority of the whole—certainly understood that no proper division of local from federal authority, nor any part of the Constitution, forbade the Federal Government to control slavery in the federal territories; while all the rest probably had the same understanding. Such, unquestionably, was the understanding of our fathers who framed the original Constitution; and the text affirms that they understood the question "better than we." (Lincoln 523)

Later, in the dramatic concluding half of the speech, Lincoln addresses the South directly, less as a conciliator than as a prosecuting attorney. In this segment, Lincoln avers that the *real* purpose of the South's position on slavery in the territories is not to uphold a Constitutional right, but to place sectional over national interests—in effect, to undermine the Union. In this section of his speech, Lincoln's conclusion about the *real* intent of the founding fathers has itself become the device, one by which the South's *real* motive is revealed:

> Your purpose, then, plainly stated, is that you will destroy the Government, unless you be allowed to construe and enforce the Constitution as you please, on all points of dispute between you and us. You will rule or ruin in all events. (Lincoln 532)

The South is not merely unpatriotic; it is immoral as well. In a final dissociation between the political and the moral, the South's conviction that slavery is right is seen as the *real* reason for its intransigence:

> [What] will convince [the South]? This and this only: cease to call slavery *wrong*, and join them in calling it *right*. And this must be done thoroughly—done in *acts* as well as in *words*. Silence will not be tolerated—we must place ourselves avowedly with them. (Lincoln 535)

Accordingly, at the conclusion of the Cooper Institute Address, Lincoln declares moral war on the South: "LET US HAVE FAITH THAT RIGHT MAKES MIGHT, AND IN THAT FAITH, LET US, TO THE END, DARE DO OUR DUTY AS WE UNDERSTAND IT" (Lincoln 536). This conclusion is the fitting terminus of his chain of dissociations.[3] For Lincoln rhetoric has become, primarily, a mode of truth, a way of sharing his moral vision with his audience.

Dissociation and Science

That dissociation is also central to the arguments scientists make is a natural extension of Perelman and Olbrechts-Tyteca's views. Science makes sense of the incompatibilities our senses reveal to us. Salt is a white crystalline substance; it is also rock-salt, a translucent substance that consists of larger crystals. When we place salt in water, it disappears. When we decompose it chemically, salt turns into equal parts of a metal, sodium, and a gas, chlorine. Science makes sense of these incompatibilities by dissociating the world we experience from the world that it reveals; in each case, the incompatibilities of our ordinary experience are replaced by a new reality, consistent with itself and with our experience. We may complete this analogy to Perelman and Olbrechts-Tyteca's insight by asserting that in each case, also, the device by which these "deceptions" of our senses are revealed is the scientific method, one in a class of means by which science discovers its truths. Such devices have in their respective fields a status analogous to dialectic in Plato's philosophy. All, in Perelman's and Olbrechts-Tyteca's terms, are rhetorical.

It is not unusual for the dissociations of science to be plainly visible, even on the surface of its prose. In our first selection, from mathematical physics, Einstein notes an apparent incompatibility between the constant speed of light and the principle that velocities are additive. We expect that a jet traveling five hundred miles an hour is really traveling five hundred and fifty miles an hour if it is followed by a fifty-mile-an-hour tail wind. Why should light be different? Why should it be a constant? The solution to this dilemma is the special theory of relativity, a theory that dissociates the concepts of space and time from their confused existence in classical mechanics:

> At this juncture the theory of relativity entered the arena. As a result of an analysis of the physical conceptions of space and time, it became evident that *in reality there is not the least incompatibility between the principle of relativity and the law of the propagation of light* and that by systematically holding fast to both these laws a logically rigid theory could be arrived at. The theory has been called the *special theory of relativity*. (20)

Our next example, from biology, is the famous last paragraph of *Origin of Species*, summarizing Darwin's views of evolution:

> It is interesting to contemplate a tangled bank, clothed with the many plants of many kinds, with birds singing on the bushes, with various insects

> flitting about, and with worms crawling through the damp earth, and to reflect that these elaborately constructed forms, so different from each other, and dependent upon each other in so complex a manner have all been produced by laws acting around us. These laws, taken in the largest sense, being Growth and Reproduction; Inheritance which is almost implied by reproduction; Variability from the indirect and direct action of the conditions of life, and from use and disuse: A Ratio of Increase so high as to lead to a Struggle for Life, and as a consequence to Natural Selection, entailing Divergence of Character and the Extinction of less-improved forms. Thus, from the war of nature, from famine and death, the most exalted object which we are capable of conceiving, namely, the production of the higher animals, directly follows. (Darwin 484)

In this passage, Darwin sees through the incompatibilities of the "tangled bank" to the orderly reality behind it: the lawful process by which evolutionary progress is assured. Influenced by the fossil record and the geographical distribution of animals and plants, and guided by analogies to artificial selection and to Malthusian theories of the limits on natural growth in populations, Darwin has derived natural selection, the law that entails evolutionary progress.

Dissociation in Philosophy

While the dissociation of concepts is useful in the analysis of political argument and science, Perelman and Olbrechts-Tyteca's central insight concerns philosophy; philosophy, they aver, arrives at its truths precisely through dissociation. It is their view that philosophical argument is *essentially* dissociative. The claim is a strong one: "Any new philosophy presupposes the working out of a conceptual apparatus, at least part of which, that which is fundamentally original, results from a dissociation of notions that enables the problems the philosopher has set for himself to be solved. It is for this reason, among others, that we consider the study of the techniques of dissociation to be so significant" (414).

We need to note that this claim modifies Perelman and Olbrechts-Tyteca's view of dissociation, cited earlier. While philosophers may be prompted by incompatibilities analogous to those in science and politics, it is far more likely that their dissociations will be triggered by problems that they themselves set. This is certainly the case with those with whom we will now deal, uniformly prompted to dissociation by what they consider the deceptiveness of a received view of the world. Perelman and Olbrechts-Tyteca call each of the dissociations through which, they contend, all philosophies are constructed, a philosophical pair, consisting of two terms, Term I, the term to be devalued, and Term II, the term to be privileged. Their prototypical philosophical pair is

appearance
reality

According to the Belgians, this pair of opposites operates throughout Western philosophy. For Plato, the world around us is only an appearance; only the Forms are real. For Locke, sights and sounds are appearances, perceptions of the secondary qualities of matter; only primary qualities, such as extension, are real; for Marx, the socio-economic system we see around us is an appearance, the superstructure; only the base, the dialectical struggle leading to the triumph of the proletariat, is real. In contrast, for the phenomenologist Merleau-Ponty, reversing this philosophical pair, it is these very appearances that are real; the so-called realities of Plato, Locke, and Marx are illusions. In all cases, it is Term I that is devalued, as against Term II. All of these dissociations are rhetorical; at the same time, they aim at truth. In all cases, then, rhetoric is a mode of truth. Let us see how this can be the case.

For the purposes of exemplification, we shall focus on the role of dissociation in the work of two philosophers, Plato and Descartes. At the center of Plato's *Phaedrus* is the device of dialectic, a two-stage process. The former stage of liaison "consists in seeing together things that are scattered about everywhere and collecting them in one kind . . . [. The latter stage consists in being] able to cut up each kind according to its species along its natural joints, [trying] not to splinter any part, as a bad butcher might do" (265E). The *Phaedrus* consists almost entirely of the second stage, that of dissociation: dialectic is the dissociative device on which Plato consistently leans.

The dialogue may be divided into three movements. In the first, two speeches on love are contrasted, the first written by Lysias and recited by Phaedrus, the second, spoken by Socrates. The second movement of the *Phaedrus* consists of Socrates's so-called Great Speech on the subject of love. We might be excused if at this point we identified love as the subject of the dialogue. In the final movement, however, a series of dialectical dissociations ensue that force us to revise this view. As a consequence of the first, we learn that the contrast between the initial speeches of Lysias and Socrates is not between two views of love: the real issue is not love, but the relationship of rhetoric to truth. By exemplifying the ability of rhetoric to argue on both sides of the issue, these two speeches have illustrated only its irresponsible fecundity.

In Plato's view, although rhetoricians must accommodate their speech to the abilities of their audiences, they must, in order to do this properly, initiate this process from the vantage point of the unvarnished truth. In this sense, Socrates's Great Speech illustrates rhetoric's proper use. It is the truth, adapted to the capacities and tastes of Phaedrus, its audience. The goal of the speech is instruction and inspiration: its purpose is to turn its listener into a philosopher. It is about love because love, properly construed is, in some sense, the equivalent to philosophy: "A soul that has seen the most will be planted in the seed of a man who will become a lover of wisdom or of beauty" (248d).

But in a last, startling dialectical turn, the Great Speech itself is dissociated from the truth. This is a consequence of the existence of this speech as a piece of writing that, by its nature, outlasts its occasion of utterance. In the final movement of the dialogue, Plato drives a wedge between the active search for the truth through dialectic and the futile attempt to arrest this search in writing, in "words that are as incapable of speaking in their own defense as they are of teaching the truth adequately" (276c). In other words, writing is an enemy of further intellectual progress:

> It will introduce forgetfulness into the soul of those who learn it: they will not practice using their memory because they will put their trust in writing, which is external and depends on signs that belong to others, instead of trying to remember from the inside, completely on their own. You have not discovered a potion for remembering; you provide your students the appearance of wisdom, not its reality. Your invention will enable them to hear many things without being properly taught, and they will imagine that they have come to know much while for the most part they will know nothing. And they will be difficult to get along with, since they will merely appear to be wise instead of really being so. (275b)

From the point of view of the *Phaedrus*, nothing written can represent current views; nothing written can be a mode of truth. This is the case of the dialogue itself: It models, but it is not dialectic, the highest form of intercourse of which human beings are capable (258e-259a).[4]

We are now at the end of our journey, one in which rhetoric has been defined and dismissed as a device for searching out the truth. While rhetoric may use the methods of dialectic, it is not dialectic (270e-272b). While its goal is instruction and inspiration, it cannot offer the best kind of instruction—only dialectic can do that—and it cannot be a means by which the truth may be discovered. These are Plato's terms. In Perelman and Olbrechts-Tyteca's terms, in this dialogue, rhetoric, in the guise of dialectic, has become a mode through which the discovery of truth is possible.

We now pass from Plato's *Phaedrus* to Descartes's *Third Meditation*, another use of dissociative rhetoric as a mode of truth. As is well known, Descartes launches his philosophical program with a series of skeptical arguments designed to separate us from our comfortable sense that we are in constant touch with reality. First, he questions the reliability of the senses. He has good reason to be wary of sense perception since, obviously, it sometimes deceives us. But there is another, stronger reason for doubt. Sometimes we have dreams so vivid that we confuse them with a waking state: Is it not possible, then, that our waking state is also a dream? Finally, is it not possible that there is a Deceiver, a God who allows us to infer from our sense impressions that there is a real world when, in fact, nothing exists beyond those impressions themselves?

Even in the face of these arguments, the most unsettling of which is the third, one clear and distinct belief survives, the *cogito*, the belief that I am a thinking thing. Why is this? Because the cogito is a clear and distinct idea, a technical term defined by Descartes in his *Principles of Philosophy*:

> I call a perception "clear" when it is present and accessible to the attentive mind—just as we say that we see something clearly when it is present to the eye's gaze and stimulates it with a sufficient degree of strength and accessibility. I call a perception "distinct" if, as well as being clear, it is so sharply separated from all other perceptions that it contains within itself only what is clear. (Dicker 85)

For Descartes, clear and distinct ideas are immune to skeptical doubt.

But even if I am sure that I exist as a thinking thing—and how can I deny this proposition without affirming it?—I cannot be sure that I am not deceived when I think I am in touch with the world as it really is. The Deceiver argument makes it imperative that the idea of God be clear and distinct: "I must examine whether there is a God, and if there is, whether he can be a deceiver. For if I do not know this, it seems that I can never be quite certain about anything else" (Dicker 74). Because of the Deceiver argument, only the existence of God can halt Descartes's skeptical regression and affirm the power of human beings to know themselves and the world.

Fortunately, by natural light, that is, clearly and distinctly, I have an idea of a "supreme God, eternal, infinite, [immutable], omniscient, omnipotent and creator of all things that exist apart from him" (77). But does this image I have correspond to anything real outside of myself? Indeed, it does:

> It is clear to me, by the natural light, that the ideas in me are like [pictures, or] images which can easily fall short of the perfection of the things from which they are taken, but which cannot contain anything greater or more perfect.
>
> The longer and more carefully I examine all these points, the more clearly and distinctly I recognize their truth. But what is my conclusion to be? If the objective reality of any of my ideas turns out to be so great that I am sure the same reality does not reside in me . . . and hence that I myself cannot be its cause, it will necessarily follow that I am not alone in the world, but that some other thing which is the cause of this idea also exists. (Dicker 78).

While "it is true that I have the idea of substance in me in virtue of the fact that I am a substance . . . this would not account for my having the idea of an infinite substance, when I am finite, unless this idea proceeded from some substance which was really infinite" (79–80). Moreover, the God that gives me the idea of God as a perfect being cannot be a deceiver, "since it is manifest by the natural light that all fraud and deception depend on some defect" (82). It is thus that Descartes's systematic skepticism is halted; it has turned into a device, a means for affirming the self and the world, and may be discarded forthwith.

In accordance with Perelman and Olbrecht-Tyteca's insight, whatever philosopher we study, we shall find that devices and dissociations are coincident with his originality (414). The Belgians purport to have discovered something essential about the nature of philosophical argument. The dissociations of Plato and Descartes certainly coincide exactly with what constitutes the originality of each philosopher. For Plato this is the dissociation between false and true rhetoric, and, more importantly, between true rhetoric, a means of conveying the truth as we understand it at any one time, and dialectic, a timeless means of discovering the truth. For Descartes, there is the dissociation, first, between our unsure sense of ourselves and of the world, as revealed to our five senses, and our sure sense of ourselves as thinking things. There is also the dissociation between confused and indistinct ideas and clear and distinct ideas, especially our clear and distinct idea of God as a guarantor of a world our unaided senses can never guarantee.

There is an instructive difference between Plato's device, and systematic skepticism, the device Descartes uses as a means to truth in his *Meditations*.

For Descartes, systematic skepticism is a temporary expedient, to be discarded once the criteria for certainty have been discovered. For Plato, while dialectic, as a means, is certainly to be devalued in relationship to its end, its liaisons and dissociations are nevertheless permanent and inseparable partners in the search for truth.

The exact status of the device by which Plato's and Descartes's dissociations are managed is crucial to understanding their philosophical significance. To Perelman and Olbrechts-Tyteca, all dissociative arguments are, along with the devices they employ, rhetorical; nevertheless, in the cases of Plato and Descartes, as in the case of all philosophers, dissociative arguments and the devices they employ are also modes of truth.

Science, Philosophy and Public Address Compared

So far, our argument puts science, philosophy, and public address more or less on a rhetorical par. But it seems mistaken not to contrast these three very different forms of discourse. Perelman suggests a distinction:

> In philosophy, one does not try to establish facts but one argues for them, in such a way, however, as to claim that this kind of reasoning should be admitted by everyone. Were it not for this claim, it would be difficult to distinguish the philosophical discourse, from the political, legal, or theological one. ("Reply " 137)

It may be objected that to say that philosophers (and scientists) aim at truth puts them on pedestals of our own making. But to assert this is to misconstrue the issue. The point is rhetorical, not epistemological. In Perelman and Olbrechts-Tyteca's terms, while politicians address particular audiences characterized by relatively parochial views, philosophers (and scientists) address a universal audience consisting of all human beings in so far as they are rational (31–35). Again, in their terms, while politicians persuade, philosophers and scientists convince (26–31). Speaking rhetorically, the concern for us is not whether these different discourses are true, but whether, primarily, their arguments have truth as their ultimate aim, their *telos*. This aim may even change over time. Lincoln's Cooper Institute Address is, as Mohrmann and Leff point out, "campaign oratory" whose "central concern is ingratiation" (177). But, regardless of what the speech was, for us today it is primarily a philosophical statement: "What would be recalled through the ages," Zarefsky writes of the Address, "was not Lincoln's legalistic deference to a historical document but his forthright defense of individual rights" (243). Exactly; the Address speaks to us neither because of its historically situated legalistic argument nor because of its original identity primarily as campaign oratory. It has a new identity appropriate to its eloquence. Now it convinces; now it aims at a universal audience.

Other distinctions need to be made. Political rhetoric contrasts with its philosophical counterpart in the heavy dependence of the former on our conviction that the public speech of politicians and their public actions must cohere, must form an integrated whole.[5] That Heidegger joined the Nazi party can be held against him, but not against his philosophy, except by those who believe, mistakenly, that *Being and Time* is surreptitiously ideological. The salient coherence lies within this work, not between it and the man who wrote it. In the case of Heidegger, we can dissociate speech from public action without serious moral penalty.

Finally, philosophy and science contrast in that, while the dissociations of science almost invariably displace one another, those of philosophy tend to persist from generation to generation: While light is no longer the alteration in a medium that it was for Aristotle or the minute spheres it was for Newton, the dissociations of Plato and Descartes are still capable of provoking philosophical discussion.

Before we conclude, we need to reapply ourselves to the question of Johnstone's with which this chapter began: We need to ask whether rhetoric is primarily a technique or primarily a mode of truth. To this question, there is no general answer, as Johnstone asserted. There is no general logic of dissociation or, we may safely add, of any other rhetorical device: Rhetoric is by definition situational. Antony's speech is a triumph of technique, of manipulation. Nevertheless, a truth is seriously at issue for him, the parochial truth that his friend has been murdered and must be avenged. A truth is also at issue for Shakespeare, a parochial truth about the dangers of regicide. In Lincoln's campaign oratory, the devices of dissociation are certainly self-serving; at the same time, they highlight the universal truth that slavery is wrong. In contrast, the devices and dissociations of the *Phaedrus* and the *Meditations* aim at universal truth without equivocation; this is also the case in the sciences. In addition, the rhetoric of *The New Rhetoric* aims at universal truth without equivocation; it is basically a philosophical discourse devoted to the claim that "only the existence of an argumentation that is neither compelling nor arbitrary can give meaning to human freedom, a state in which a reasonable choice can be exercised" (514). Finally, Johnstone's own rhetoric is aimed at universal truth without equivocation; his dissociation between rhetoric as a mode of truth and as a technique is meant as a contribution to the elucidation of a still salient philosophical question.

We may summarize by saying that Perelman and Olbrechts-Tyteca have made a genuine contribution to our understanding of the way philosophers argue. Their deceptively simple pairing of device and dissociation yields a rich harvest when applied to works as different as those of Plato and Descartes. Devices as different as dialectic in the first case and systematic skepticism in the second reveal exactly the points at which philosophers define themselves against the traditions to which they belong; it is these dissociations that define their originality and, simultaneously, their rhetorical essence, as Perelman and Olbrechts-Tyteca predict. Moreover, their notions of device and dissociation can be generalized to apply to public address and to the sciences, applications that they do not consider.

CHAPTER 8

Arrangement as Persuasion

Although each of the five faculties that comprise ancient rhetoric—invention, arrangement, style, delivery, and memory—must have a purpose in persuasion, it is by no means clear, with any faculty but invention, how that persuasive purpose is realized. Arrangement is a case in point. There is much talk about the arrangements appropriate to classical oratory, but little explanation of how form can have a persuasive influence separate from though in conjunction with content. Perelman and Olbrechts-Tyteca address this problem: Their solution amounts to a theory of arrangement. In this chapter, we will outline this theory. While expository clarity dictates that we deal initially only with parts of discourses, this focus pays scant attention to the architectonic ambitions of arrangement—a canon that deals, centrally, with the *whole* of discourses. In recognition of the larger purpose we deal, in the second part of this chapter, with these wholes, not only in public address, but in philosophy and in the sciences. We do this to demonstrate the scope of the Belgians' theory. We shall see that in these very different types of discourse, arrangement functions differently, though persuasively.

Perelman and Olbrechts-Tyteca underline the persuasive importance of arrangement when they say: "The conditioning of the audience . . . is also brought about by the discourse. A speech does not leave the hearer the same as he was at the beginning. On the other hand, it does not change his beliefs irresistibly, as would the steps in a demonstration. The order adopted is crucial precisely because the changes in the audience are both effective and contingent" (491). Perelman and Olbrechts-Tyteca's taxonomy of the changes that order can influence is threefold. Audiences can be influenced concerning the arguments they will logically accept; audiences may also change their attitude toward those arguments. Third, arrangement has a goal tied to self-reference, one in which the audience's consciousness of a particular arrangement is the basis of its increased receptivity to the speaker's message. In this last case, arrangement is persuasive because it is perceived—a perception that in itself leads to conviction.

Cross-examination is the paradigm example of Perelman's contention that the arrangement of arguments is a means of persuasion. Here is an excerpt from Clarence Darrow's cross-examination of William Jennings Bryan in the Scopes trial, an adjudication concerning the legality of teaching evolution in the state of Tennessee:

DARROW You have never had any interest in the age of the various races and people and civilization and animals that exist upon the earth today? Is that right?

BRYAN I have never felt a great deal of interest in the effort that has been made to dispute the Bible by the speculations of men, or the investigations of men.

❄ ❄ ❄

DARROW You do know that there are thousands of people who profess to be Christians who believe the earth is much more ancient and that the human race is much more ancient?

BRYAN I think there may be.

DARROW And you have never investigated to find out how long man has been on earth?

BRYAN I have never found it necessary.

DARROW For any reason, whatever it is?

BRYAN To examine every speculation; but if I had done it I never would have done anything else.

DARROW I ask for a direct answer?

BRYAN I do not expect to find out all those things and I do not expect to find out about races.

DARROW I didn't ask you that. Now I ask you if you know it was interesting enough, or important enough for you to try to find out about how old these ancient civilizations were?

BRYAN No, I have not made a study of it.

DARROW Don't you know that the ancient civilizations of China are 6,000 or 7,000 years old, at the very least?

BRYAN No, but they would not run back beyond the creation, according to the Bible, 6,000 years.

DARROW You don't know how old they are, is that right?

BRYAN I don't know how old they are, but probably you do. (Laughter in the courtyard). I think you would give the preference to anybody who opposed the Bible, and I give the preference to the Bible.

DARROW I see. Well, you are welcome to your opinion. Have you any idea how old the Egyptian civilization is? (*The World's Most Famous Court Trial* 290–91)

In cross-examination we see the persuasive purpose of order at every step of the way. In this exchange, Darrow is trying to maneuver Bryan into revealing the inconsistency of his position. At every stage, Darrow controls the pace and process by which the revelation is made. At various points, Bryan attempts to change the direction of the questioning in his favor, but to no avail. Darrow relentlessly returns to the point—his point. Darrow's technique is simple and deadly. He asks Bryan about the age of civilizations that are, apparently, older than the Creation. Bryan's responses can then be reconstructed by an audience as a continuous discourse demonstrating that to hold such views is to be inconsistent with oneself. The effectiveness of Darrow's maneuver derives from a necessary condition of any sound reasoning: that it be consistent.

The Platonic dialogues are the example of cross-examination mentioned by Perelman and Olbrechts-Tyteca (493). Since they are fictional, however, they lack the requisite resistance on the part of the respondent, a resistance that is integral to the persuasiveness of such testimony. In this cross-examination from a real trial, Bryan reveals an inconsistency between accepted views of the age of the earth and his views, despite his best efforts to prevent such an outcome. Bryan's open admission would not have served Darrow's purposes better: Darrow's task was at a minimum to *reveal* the inconsistency in Bryan's views to a jury, *despite* his resistance. The Belgians comment on this procedure: "It is an indubitable advantage to the person arguing to be able to put the questions of his choice, and to choose the order in which they are to be put. The efficaciousness of the Socratic method [as of cross-examination] depends on the skillful use of this privilege" (492–93).

Cross-examination is a special case of managing change in the arguments audiences will logically accept, Perelman and Olbrechts-Tyteca's first category, a special case in which interrogators use the freedom the law gives them to undermine opposing positions. In the normal case in public address, speakers manage refutation themselves. In his Cooper Institute Address, Lincoln's purpose is to undermine claims that the spread of slavery to the territories is constitutional. Such claims were grounded on two of the first ten amendments of the Constitution: an amendment that protects property, and one that bestows upon the states and the people rights not specified as federal. Lincoln chooses not to argue Constititional law, wisely, in view of the recent pro-slavery Dred Scott decision by the Supreme Court. Instead, he begins with a claim on which both he and his chief opponent, Stephen Douglas, unquestionably agree, namely, that "*our fathers, when they framed the Government under which we live, understood this question just as well, and even better, than we do now*" (Lincoln 517; his emphasis). Lincoln then marshalls the historical evidence in his favor: the founding fathers, the framers of the Constitution on which the government is based, by and large voted *against* the expansion of slavery to the territories (Lincoln 523). Only when the fact of his agreement with Douglas has been displayed, and its inconsistency with the position Douglas holds on slavery has been established, does Lincoln turn to the amendments to the Constitution:

> Is it not a little presumptuous in any one at this day to affirm that the two things [the Constitution and its amendments] which that Congress deliberately framed, and carried to maturity at the same time, are absolutely inconsistent with each other? And does not such affirmation become impudently absurd when coupled with the other affirmation from the same mouth, that those who did the two things, alleged to be inconsistent, understood whether they really were inconsistent better than we—better than he who affirms that they are inconsistent? (Lincoln 524)

The order of these arguments is crucial: The history of voting records must be established before the argument from consistency makes sense. Perelman and Olbrechts-Tyteca comment: "Since, as a general rule, the laying of firm premises is a prime consideration in argumentation, it will not be disputed that the statement of facts will be advantageously placed at the beginning of a discourse, since the facts command the largest measure of agreement" (494).

In their discussion of the effect of arrangement on attitudinal force, their second category, Perelman and Olbrechts-Tyteca focus on two topics: the *exordium* or introduction of the speech, and its *confirmatio* or body. The Belgians are especially concerned to show that "the introduction is indispensable to the persuasive effect of the discourse" (496). This indispensability holds even when some introductory functions are assigned to someone other than the speaker: "The introduction of the speaker by the chairman of a meeting has no other purpose than to make it unnecessary for the speaker to sing his own praises" (498). In effect, in such cases an attitudinal function has been allocated to another, prior speaker.

Perelman and Olbrechts-Tyteca concur with the traditional advice that in exordiums speakers ought to render their audiences receptive, attentive, and well-disposed. An audience is receptive to the extent that it is open to instruction, an openness that depends on the salience of the issue before it. An audience is attentive if it is centered on what speakers have to say, a centering that depends on the extent to which the salience of the issue is rendered immediate. An audience is well-disposed to the extent that it is inclined to agree with the speakers' point of view, an inclination that depends initially on the coincidence of the initial positions of speakers and audiences. The exordium of Lincoln's House Divided speech, given at the close of the Republican State Convention in Springfield, Illinois on June 16, 1858, exemplifies a concern for each of these three purposes:

> If we could first know *where* we are, and *whither* we are tending, we could better judge *what* to do, and *how* to do it.
> We are now far into the *fifth* year, since a policy was initiated, with the *avowed* object, and *confident* promise, of putting an end to slavery agitation.
> Under the operation of that policy, that agitation has not only, *not ceased*, but has *constantly augmented*.
> In my opinion, it *will* not cease, until a *crisis* shall have been reached, and passed—
> "A house divided against itself cannot stand."
> I believe that this government cannot endure, permanently, half *slave* and half *free*.
> I do not expect the Union to be *dissolved*—I do not expect the house to *fall*—but I *do* expect it will cease to be divided.
> It will become *all* one thing, or *all* the other.
> Either the *opponents* of slavery, will arrest the further spread of it, and place it where the public mind shall rest in the belief that it is in course of ultimate extinction; or its *advocates* will push it forward, till it shall become alike lawful in *all* the States, *old* as well as *new*—*North* as well as *South*.
> Have we no *tendency* to the latter condition? (Lincoln 372–373; Lincoln's emphasis)

For Lincoln, the primary purpose of this exordium is to arrest the attention of its audience by presenting them with a salient issue in dramatic form. In this case, Lincoln need not be concerned overmuch with receptivity. And he can assume salience, just as he can assume that his audience will be inclined to believe that the pro-slavery faction has national ambitions. All speakers must be concerned with all three purposes, though not every exordium need address all three, since at times some can be assumed.

In addressing the attitudinal force of arrangement, Perelman and Olbrechts-Tyteca also focus on the order of arguments in the *confirmatio*. This is not the *logical* order of the confirmatio, the one concerned with the rational acceptance of premises; rather, this is the *psychological* order, the one concerned with the audience's disposition to accept the speaker's arguments.

Cicero's fourth oration against the rebellious Catiline clarifies the important distinction between the logical and psychological orders of the speech. In this oration, Cicero wants to convince the Senate that all ranks will support a decision to execute the conspirators. He begins his catalogue of support with the equestrian order, then moves to the freedmen, and finally to the slaves: "There is not one slave," he says, "—provided, only, that the condition of his bondage is tolerable—who is not aghast at the effrontery of citizens, who does not want to preserve the status, who does not dare with might and main to do his part for the common welfare" (155). At this juncture, Cicero relates an anecdote that gives this last point a dramatic presence:

> You have, no doubt, been intrigued by the story that is making the rounds of how a certain operator in the pay of Lentulus went dashing about to the various shops here in the forum. He hoped he could subvert, for a price, the souls of the needy and unskilled laborers, and started on the project by approaching many of them. But he found no takers for his offer, either among men who were hard-pressed or among men who had discarded their sense of loyalty. There was not a single one who did not prefer the security of the very work-bench he occupied, of the place where he earned his daily wage for work done, of his own tiny bedroom and cot, and the peaceful pace of his own life. (156)

Why does Cicero use the power of arangement, the natural presence that ultimate placement provides, to emphasize the support of slaves over that of other social orders? Because, in Cicero's judgment, support of the Senate is best guaranteed when even those who have the least appreciation of the real issues, and the least to gain or lose by the Senate's action, instinctively and wholeheartedly turn away from the Catilinarian conspiracy.

Arrangement also has a persuasive force founded in self-reference, Perelman and Olbrechts-Tyteca's third category. For a speaker to achieve this effect, the audience must be made conscious that the content of the speech is ordered in a way that is "natural." The Belgians' paradigm example of such an order is the chronological: "The observance of chronological order in the relation of facts is the most chararacteristic example of . . . [a] 'natural order'," an example of a form that is "easily grasped" and that, simultaneously, "satisf[ies] the understanding" (503).

While, for Perelman and Olbrechts-Tyteca, the chronological is the model of natural order, other orders can have an analogous effect: "Oratorical custom can also provide schemes which constitute *patterns*, and so seem to be external to any particular speech. Particularly in continuous discourse, we find it difficult to distinguish what part is attributable to habit or custom when the speech strikes us as corresponding to a normal order" (503; their emphasis). Taken together, the five sections of the classical oration—exordium or introduction, narratio or statement of facts, confirmatio or proof, refutatio or refutation, and peroratio or conclusion—constitute an example of an order that can be perceived as natural by those, like the Romans, who are habituated to that particular form of public address.

The attitudinal force of this habitual form of Roman public address is perhaps most conspicuous when its conventions are violated for dramatic effect. In his first oration against Catiline, Cicero does not give us the emotionally calm, audience-ingratiating exordium recommended by the handbooks; instead, he asks a series of rhetorical questions, each more heated than the last:

> How long, Catiline, how long, I say, will you keep wearing down our patience? How long will that raving madness of yours baffle us? How long will that wild arrogance you glory in last? Is it nothing to you that the Palatine is now guarded at night? Nothing that the city is protected by patrols, nothing that the people are panic-stricken, nothing that loyal citizens have formed a solid front against you, nothing that this very meeting place of the Senate is strongly fortified? Do you take no notice whatsoever of the looks on the faces of all these men? Do you not realize that all your plans have been exposed? Can you not see that your conspiracy is now held in check by the simple fact that all the Senators met here have accurate knowledge of it? What one of us, do you think, is not fully aware of what you did last night, and the night before last, of where you were, of who was with you, of what plans you laid? (106–107)

The dramatic effect of this exordium depends on the audience's perception that a normal expectation has been violated and on their inference from this violation that there is an immediate danger to the state.

But a "natural" order may also be created by the speech itself. Lincoln's House Divided speech provides us with an excellent example of the invention of such an order. Following the exordium to his House Divided speech, just analyzed, Lincoln begins with a narrative of the pro-slavery Nebraska bill and of the pro-slavery Dred Scott decision, a sequence of actions apparently unrelated. Lincoln then tells us what this narrative means:

> We cannot absolutely *know* that all these exact adaptations are the result of preconcert. But when we see a lot of framed timbers, different portions of which have been gotten out at different times and places and by different workmen—Stephen, Franklin, Roger, and James, for instance—and we see these timbers joined together, and see they exactly make the frame of a house or a mill, all the tenons and mortises exactly fitting, and all the lengths and proportions of the different pieces exactly adapted to their respected places, and not a piece too many or too few—not omitting even scaffolding—or, if a single piece be lacking, we see the place in the frame exactly fitted and prepared to yet bring such a piece in—in *such* a case we find it impossible not to *believe* that Stephen and Franklin and Roger and James all understood one another from the beginning, and all worked upon a common *plan* or *draft* drawn up before the first lick was struck. (Lincoln 377; Lincoln's emphasis)

This striking analogy turns the conclusions Lincoln is reaching into the inevitable result of a "natural" order, one that gives to his narrative the sinister shape of a conspiracy.

Arrangement in Whole Discourses

We will now examine the persuasive power of arrangement in three complete discourses—Lincoln's Second Inaugural, Descartes's first *Meditation*, and a scientific article, one in which two biochemists, Stuart Brody and Charles Yanofsky, elucidate the mechanism by which mutations alter protein structure. In these exercises in public address, philosophy, and science, we will analyze the persuasive effect of the arrangement of whole discourses. They will show that the Belgians' theory of arrangement has a wide scope.

In his Second Inaugural, Lincoln's exordium is studied, cool, and impersonal. Not until its final sentence does he venture into the first person plural (referring to the nation that he leads), and the first person singular (referring, of course, to himself):

> At this second appearing to take the oath of presidential office, there is less occasion for an extended address than there was at the first. Then a statement, somewhat in detail, of a course to be pursued, seemed fitting and proper. Now, at the expiration of four years, during which public declarations

> have been constantly called forth on every point and phase of the great contest which still absorbs the attention, and engrosses the energies of the nation, little that is new could be presented. The progress of our arms, upon which all else chiefly depends, is as well known to the public as to myself; and it is, I trust, reasonably satisfactory and encouraging to all. With high hope for the future, no prediction in regard to it is ventured. (Lincoln 792)

This deliberate flatness may seem counterproductive. But Lincoln—a national leader in a time of national crisis—needs no art to make his audience receptive, well-disposed, or attentive. Moreover, as it turns out, this flatness forms the imperturbable base out of which arises an arc, simultaneously logical and psychological. In his second paragraph, Lincoln reveals that this exordium is not merely expository; it has also tacitly initiated a narrative whose thesis is that the war is an effect of the South's greater propensity for belligerence, egged on by "insurgent agents":

> On the occasion corresponding to this four years ago, all thoughts were anxiously directed to an impending civil war. All dreaded it—all sought to avert it. While the inaugural address was being delivered from this place, devoted altogether to *saving* the Union without war, insurgent agents were in the city seeking to *destroy* it without war—seeking to dissolve the Union, and divide effects, by negotiation. Both parties deprecated war; but one of them would *make* war rather than let the nation survive; and the other would *accept* war rather than let it perish. And the war came. (Lincoln 792; Lincoln's emphasis)

In his third and penultimate paragraph, Lincoln shifts dramatically from a political to a moral universe, a universe in which the South's position on slavery merits condemnation:

> One eighth of the whole population were colored slaves, not distributed generally over the Union, but localized in the Southern part of it. These slaves constituted a peculiar and powerful interest. All knew that this interest was, somehow, the cause of the war. To strengthen, perpetuate, and extend this interest was the object for which the insurgents would rend the Union, even by war; while the government claimed no right to do more than restrict the territorial enlargement of it. Neither party expected for the war, the magnitude, or the duration, which it has already attained. Neither anticipated that the *cause* of the conflict might cease with, or even before, the conflict itself should cease. Each looked for an easier triumph, and a result less fundamental and astounding. Both read the same Bible, and pray to the same God; and each invokes His aid against the other. It may seem strange that any men should dare to ask a just God's assistance in wringing their bread from the sweat of other men's faces; but let us judge

> not that we be not judged. The prayers of both could not be answered; that of neither has been answered fully. The Almighty has his own purposes. "Woe unto the world because of offences! for it must needs be that offences come; but woe to that man by whom the offence cometh!" If we shall suppose that American Slavery is one of those offences which, in the providence of God, must needs come, but which, having continued through His appointed time, He now wills to remove, and that He gives to both North and South, this terrible war, as the woe due to those by whom the offence came, shall we discern therein any departure from those divine attributes, which the believers in a Living God always ascribe to Him? Fondly do we hope—fervently do we pray—that this mighty scourge of war may speedlily pass away. Yet, if God wills that it continue, until all the wealth piled by the bond-man's two hundred and fifty years of unrequited toil shall be sunk, and until every drop of blood drawn by the lash, shall be paid by another drawn with the sword, as was said three thousand years ago, so still it must be said "the judgments of the Lord, are true and righteous altogether." (Lincoln 792–793; Lincoln's emphasis)

In his peroration, in the most dramatic move of all, Lincoln shifts without apparent logical or psychological transition from the indignation he has just displayed to the forgiveness he thinks is now appropriate:

> With malice toward none; with charity for all; with firmness in the right as God gives us to see the right, let us strive on to finish the work we are in; to bind up the nation's wounds; to care for him who shall have borne the battle, and for his widow, and his orphan—to do all which may achieve and cherish a just and lasting peace, among ourselves, and with all nations. (Lincoln 793)

The logical gap between indignation and forgiveness makes sense only if it is bridged by an enthymeme natural to Christians—Christians forgive their enemies; therefore, the North should forgive the South. As a consequence of this enthymematic link—the consequence of the need of Christians to identify themselves as Christians—Lincoln can present a conciliatory attitude toward the South as a natural inference from agreed-upon premises. This effect is enhanced by Lincoln's refusal to distribute responsibility for the war to the whole of the South. Not only are "insurgents" identified twice as the culprits; "this terrible war" is visited equally on North and South, apparently as a punishment for the founding of a republic whose dedication to liberty has been marred by the continuing presence of slavery.

But so far we have spoken only of one sort of order. The arrangement of Lincoln's Second Inaugural is persuasive, finally, because it is organized according to four dovetailing principles of order, each external to it and, to that extent, natural. The order of the speech is canonical in that it moves from *exordium* through the *confirmatio* to the *peroratio;* the order is chronological in that it follows the course of the Civil War and projects the consequences of that war into the near future; the order is causal in that it sees the war as an effect of Southern belligerence (fomented, to be sure, by insurgents), and a just peace as an effect of Northern forgiveness; the order is Christian in that it moves naturally from indignation to forgiveness.

We now move from politics to philosophy; in philosophy as well arrangement has persuasive force. In his *First Meditation,* Descartes's progress to hyperbolic doubt also follows an order that is simultaneously logical, attitudinal, and self-referential. First of all, he argues; he establishes that the senses can be an unreliable guide to reality; after all, dreams are sometimes as vivid as the experiences of waking life, and "there are never any sure signs by means of which being awake can be distinguished from being asleep" (10). But this insight is insufficient to justify hyperbolic doubt: The fact that dreams jumble up such qualities as shape, quantity, size, place, and time attests, after all, to the existence of such qualities. Moreover, mathematics and logic exist, even in dreams; even in dreams, two and three make five. But let us suppose for the sake of argument that our perceptions of the world are under the control, not of a benevolent God, but of "some malicious demon" (12). If this is the case, can anything be certain? We have arrived at hyperbolic doubt.

Descartes's progress to hyperbolic doubt follows a parallel attitudinal order, an order whose purpose is also to undermine the structures of ordinary experience. The logical arrangement of Descartes's argument is coincident with a series of progressively unsettling images designed to provide that logic with attitudinal support. He speaks of his need "to demolish everything completely and start again right from the foundations" (9). While he differentiates himself from "madmen, whose brains are so damaged by melancholia that they firmly maintain they are kings when they are paupers," nevertheless, he is forced to agree that he has "all the same experiences while asleep as madmen do when awake" (10). He concludes that he is "like a prisoner who is enjoying an imaginary freedom while asleep; as he begins to suspect he is asleep, he dreads being woken up" (12).

Descartes's reflections also persuade self-referentially, that is, through their identity as a genre: the meditation. Descartes is heir to several meditative traditions. But, despite differences among these, all share a common nature: They are not so much a record of, as an invitation to, experience. They persuade, not so much by what they say, as by their power to lead the reader through a series of experiences. To read the *Meditations*, then, is not so much to submit to Descartes's instruction as to participate in a tradition of meditation with Descartes as one's guide. To those familiar with it, the meditational order—which represents a spiritual journey as a chronological and argumentative one—will be perceived as natural and persuasive because it is what it is (Rorty 1–20). As Descartes says:

> I rightly demand special attention on the part of my readers, and have purposely chosen a special style of writing which I considered most suitable for this aim. . . . I think it quite fair to ignore altogether and despise as of no weight the criticisms of people who are unwilling to meditate with me and instead persist in holding their preconceived views. I know how difficult it is for anyone—even someone who gives it his full attention and who is really trying to discover the truth—to keep before his mind the whole compass of my *Meditations* and at the same time grasp each part, both of which must, in my opinion, be achieved if the full point of my work is to be comprehended. (Letter quoted in Rorty 1)

Arrangement is also an important aspect of persuasion in science. The introduction to a typical experimental article, Brody and Yanofsky's "Suppressor Gene Alteration of Protein Primary Structure," initiates an order founded on logic:

> Some suppressor genes are known to act by restoring an enzymatic activity that is specfiically lacking in a mutant strain. This could be accomplished in many ways, with or without the alteration of the enzyme in question.[1–3] Suppressor mutations have been detected which affect the A protein of the trytophan synthetase of *Escherichia coli*. Previous studies have shown that alterations in the primary structure of this protein can result in forward mutation,[4, 5] reverse mutation,[6] and recombination[6] within the structural gene (the A gene) for this protein. The present paper indicates that a suppressor mutation in a region of the genome distant from the A gene also leads to a change in the primary structure of the A protein. (In Brody 634)

As John Swales has noticed, such introductions have a canonical form: The introduction establishes a research space, indicates a niche in that space suitable for the claim, and, finally, occupies that niche with the claim. In this particular article, the research space is the interaction of genes and proteins, at the time of this article at the cutting edge of molecular genetics. The niche is the causal role of the suppressor genes, current research made plausible and salient by research in the immediate past, as the many citations indicate. Brody and Yanofsky occupy that niche with their claim that a mutation in the gene is causally related to a change in the structure of the protein.

Within this framework, they construct a logical argument. Brody and Yanofsky's claim determines their choice of Materials and Methods for experimentation, the subject of their next section. When methods are applied to materials, experimental results are obtained. While the claim concerns the causal role of suppressor genes, the support for that claim, the experiments detailed in the Results section of the article, concerns only quantities that can be measured, "differences in heat- or acid-stability" of otherwise closely related peptides (Brody 635), differences tacitly assumed to operationalize such causal claims. When in their Results section Brody and Yanofsky state that these experiments prove "that amino acid replacement occurs in the A protein as a result of the action of the suppressor gene" (638), they are assuming the full efficacy of this operationalization.

The Discussion section, invariably the last substantive section of the experimental article, attempts to explain the causal fact just established: "The results of these investigations can be most easily explained by postulating that the consequences of a mutation in a suppressor gene such as the suppressor of strain A-36 su is to produce an alteration in the specificity of incorporation of amino acids into proteins" (639). In this section, the experimenters move from fact to theory, a movement that, in this particular article, integrates the fact just discovered into the field of existing theories of protein alteration.

The attitudinal and self-referential aspects of arrangement are also important to scientific persuasion. The form of the experimental article—Introduction, Materials and Methods, Results, Discussion—is psychological as well as logical. This canonical arrangement embodies, not experimental practice, but its idealization (Latour and Woolgar 252), an idealization in which science has a strong emotional investment. It is an idealization embedded in the scientific psyche since Bacon, for whom a research program consists of "a double scale or ladder, ascendant and descendent; ascending from experiments to the invention of causes, and descending from causes to the invention of new experiments" (1962, pp. 90–91). Finally, the arrangement of the experimental article also has a self-referential aspect; it is bound to seem external and natural to scientists for whom, as a result of rigorous editorial enforcement, it is the only one possible.

Public Address, Philosophy, and Science Compared

Before we close, we need to address the question of balance among the logical, attitudinal, and self-referential aspects of arrangement in public address, philosophy, and science. In public address, these aspects are in a rough equilibrium. None is foregrounded; no one is emphasized at the expense of the others. From this we may infer that it is equally legitimate to call on any of these persuasive resources when matters of state are at stake. This does not seem to be the case in philosophy. As in public address, the logical, attitudinal, and self-referential aspects of arrangement in Descartes reinforce one another; however, in the *First Meditation*, the attitudinal aspect is very much in the background, an allocation we think may be typical of philosophical discourse.

The relative prominence of its logical and self-referential aspects brings philosophy close to science, a neighborliness appropriate to two sorts of discourse addressed to a universal audience. But the discourses of philosophy and science also differ in two important respects. Science is even less hospitable than philosophy to attitudinal display; moreover, in philosophy, though not in science, argument reigns supreme; polemic is an ever-present possibility. Though Brody and Yanofsky construct an argument, especially in their Discussion section, Perelman and Olbrechts-Tyteca are surely correct when they say that "the use of conventionally admitted experimental and deductive techniques, reduces, in science, the room for argumentation" (137). The logical orders of philosophy and science are therefore only in part coincident.

Conclusion

In this chapter we have tried to clarify and exemplify Perelman and Olbrechts-Tyteca's belief that arrangement is integral to the persuasive process. In their view, there are three persuasive aspects of arrangement. The first is logical; it concerns the order of arguments best designed for rational persuasion. The second is attitudinal; it concerns the order of arguments best designed to alter or reinforce the perspectives of audiences. The third is self-referential; it concerns the persuasive effect of the audience's perception that a particular kind of arrangement is a "natural" one, external to discourse. Each of the areas we have examined—public address, philosophy, and science—uses arrangement persuasively. While in public address, all three aspects operate with equal force, in philosophy, the logical and self-referential aspects are foregrounded, while the attitudinal aspect is firmly in the background. In the sciences, the logical and the self-referential aspects of arrangement are, apparently, the only ones present.

CHAPTER 9

The Figures as Argument

The conviction of Perelman and Olbrechts-Tyteca that style plays a supporting rather than a leading role in argument leads to their decision to treat the figures,[1] not in one place, but only as they become a factor in particular arguments. While correct conceptually, this decision is indefensible as an expository strategy because, as a consequence of its execution, their view of the figures recedes too far into the background of their text. Our goal in this chapter is to make this view visible and, in order to demonstrate its scope, to apply it to argument in public address, in philosophy and in science. Before we do so, however, we need to define the figures in Perelman and Olbrechts-Tyteca's terms, to indicate their range, and to outline the taxonomy that will form the organizational backbone of this chapter.

The object of their study is generally the figures as classically construed; for the two, figures consist of tropes and schemes. The line between them is clear in principle: tropes focus on meaning, schemes on form. "She wallows in her misery," is a trope because it applies to a human being a predicate ordinarily applied to pigs. An advertisement for plastic surgeons reads, "Your body is our business." This expression is a scheme in which the two nouns are linked by alliteration, suggesting a conceptual relationship between them, one that reinforces the trope that extends the meaning of "commercial enterprise." The line between meaning and form, however, is not always clear. Take an antithesis like "You should eat to live, not live to eat." The heart of this figure may be in the form—in this case the reversal of predicate and infinitive—but, clearly, not just any reversal will do; meaning has to be part of the definition of antithesis. This blurs the dividing line between schemes and tropes, tacitly accepted by Perelman and his co-author.

For them, the figures have a discernible structure. While this may be syntactic, semantic, or pragmatic, we always have the sense that an idea is being expressed in a way that so varies from the literal that it draws attention to itself (168). For example, alliteration (as in "Your body is our business") is a scheme with a discernible *syntactic* structure; metonymy (as in "All hands on deck") is a trope with a discernible *semantic* structure. Perelman and Olbrechts-Tyteca also include allusion and quotation among the figures. Their discernible structure is, rather, *pragmatic:* They add to the meaning of texts by linking them with companion texts of considerable cultural significance. Lincoln's many allusions to and quotations from the Bible make this sacred text a close companion to his thought and expression.

Perelman and Olbrechts-Tyteca's criteria do not always permit us to identify figures in actual texts. This is because whether something is a figure depends also on its context, and on the state of the language. Is it metaphorical to speak of the leg of a chair? Not now, but presumably before 1680, the time of the first recorded use of this expression in English. (This is not to say that such dead metaphors cannot be revived; as we shall see, the Belgians make much of this revival as a rhetorical device.) Just as state of the language matters, so does context. Is it really ever metaphoric to say that men have veins through which blood flows? No? Just observe Bacon in "Of Truth" :

> *What is Truth?* said jesting Pilate and would not wait for an answer. Certainly there be [those] that delight in giddiness, and count it as a bondage to fix a belief, affecting free-will in thinking, as well as in acting. And though the sects of philosophers of that kind be gone, yet there remain certain discoursing wits which are of the same veins, though there be not so much blood in them as was in those of the ancients. (4)

In this passage, Bacon is using blood metaphorically to compare contemporary skeptics unfavorably with their ancient counterparts.

Context is especially crucial because Perelman and Olbrechts-Tyteca's chief concern is the use of figures in the conduct of arguments: A figure is argumentative "if it brings about a change in perspective, and its use seems normal in relation to this new situation" (169). But this effect can be determined only in context: "The moment a figure is detached from its context and pigeon-holed, it is almost necessarily perceived under its least argumentative aspect" (171). This decontextualization is the primary reason, the Belgians feel, that the argumentative aspect of figures has been neglected. Accordingly, in this chapter, we cite our representative figures in a context broader than is routinely the case. We hope that this extended quotation does not try the reader's patience overmuch; it seems to us the only way to make Perelman and Olbrechts-Tyteca's point effectively.

While Perelman and Olbrechts-Tyteca define the figures, they do not specify the extent of the domain over which the figures rule; traditionally it is specified as a word, a sentence, or, at its most expansive, two or three related sentences. Their examples all conform to this traditional limitation. But, as we shall see, in our analysis of public address, philosophy, and science, this limitation is a genuine hindrance to rhetorical analysis. In our concluding section, we shall show that metaphor, at least, is a figure that can exercise its influence over texts as a whole. We suspect that the same is true of irony, synecdoche, and metonymy, those figures identified by Kenneth Burke as master tropes.

Perelman and Olbrechts-Tyteca deliberately offer no taxonomy of the figures; they feel that their principal concern is the *effect* of the figures in argumentation. In pursuit of this goal, they provide three examples of such effects: "to suggest a choice, to increase the impression of presence, . . . to bring about communion with the audience" (172). We confess to finding the effect of choice too obscure for exposition; and we find it more convenient to take up the effect of presence in the next chapter, devoted entirely to presence. The effect of communion we do take up in this chapter, making it part of our taxonomy of figures. This taxonomy is roughly coincident with the Belgians' division into figures primarily semantic, syntactic, or pragmatic: tropes, schemes, figures of communion.

We divide the primarily semantic tropes into four categories and the primarily syntactic schemes into two. In the first set of tropes are those that exaggerate, understate, or reverse meaning. Hyperbole, litotes, and irony will be our examples. Our second category consists of tropes that make comparisons between semantic fields. Metaphor and personification will be our examples. A final category consists of tropes that involve a substitution within a semantic field. Metonymy, synecdoche, ploce, and polyptoton will be our examples. Schemes we divide into two groups: those emphasizing likeness and those emphasizing difference. In the first group, anaphora, epistrophe, polysyndeton, and asyndeton are our examples; antithesis is our example of a scheme in the second group. A final category consists of primarily pragmatic figures, those that promote communion between speaker and auditor. Allusion and quotation will be our examples. In the passages we analyze, the tropes and schemes we comment on are set in italic.

Tropes That Exaggerate, Understate, or Reverse Meaning

Hyperbole. To use hyperbole is to exaggerate. In an early speech concerning the threat of mob violence, Lincoln says:

> It would be tedious, as well as useless, to recount the horrors of all [the outrages committed by mobs]. Those happening in the State of Mississippi, and at St. Louis, are, perhaps, the most dangerous in example and revolting to humanity, In the Mississippi case, they first commenced by hanging the regular gamblers; a set of men, certainly not following for a livelihood, a very useful, or very honest occupation; but one which, so far from being forbidden by the laws, was actually licensed by an act of the Legislature, passed but a single year before. Next, negroes, suspected of conspiring to raise an insurrection, were caught up and hanged in all parts of the State; then, white men, supposed to be leagued with the negroes; and finally, strangers, from neighboring States, going thither on business, were, in many instances subjected to the same fate. Thus went on the process of hanging, from gamblers to negroes, from negroes to white citizens, and from these to strangers; *till, dead men were seen literally dangling from the boughs of trees upon every roadside; and in numbers almost sufficient, to rival the native Spanish moss of the country, as a drapery of the forest.* (Lincoln 78)

Lincoln's hyperboles come at the end of a list of progressively worse outrages. They are not to be taken literally; rather, their "role is to provide a reference which draws the mind in a certain direction only to force it later to retreat a little, to the extreme limit of what seems compatible with its idea of the human, the possible, the probable" (*New Rhetoric* 291). In Lincoln's first hyperbole, auditors are to imagine men hanging from every tree, then to retreat from this number to some possible or a probable figure. In his second hyperbole, auditors are to resume the exercise, imagining the trees with men hanging from them are as numerous as trees with moss hanging from them; then to retreat to some plausible, though unspecified figure. The argumentative effect of these hyperboles is to reinforce Lincoln's claim concerning the significance and the horror of mob violence.

Litotes. To use litotes is to understate, as in this example from Douglas's opening speech at Alton:

> Now, I stand on that same platform in 1858, that I did in 1850, '54 and '56. But the Washington *Union*, pretending to be the organ of the Administration, in the number of the 5th of this month, devotes three and half columns to establish these propositions: first, that Douglas in his Freeport speech, avowed the same doctrine that he did when arguing the Nebraska

> bill on the same ground that he did Clay's measures of 1850—that he is the same now as he was in 1856, '54 and '50, and consequently never was a Democrat. Now wasn't that funny that I was never a Democrat. No pretense that I have changed a hair's breadth. The *Union* proves by my speeches that I expounded the Compromise Measures of 1850, just as I do now—that I advocated the Kansas-Nebraska bill in its passage, just as I do now—just as I did in my Freeport speech, and yet it says I am not a Democrat and cannot be trusted, because I have not changed during the whole time, Now it did occur to me that in 1854, the author of the Kansas-Nebraska bill was considered *a pretty good Democrat.* It did occur to me that in 1856, *when I was exerting every nerve and every energy* for James Buchanan, then standing on that identical platform I was on that I was *a pretty good Democrat.* (Lincoln-Douglas 335)

Litotes is understatement that intensifies meaning. It "can be set in opposition to hyperbole . . . Because, when it seeks to establish a value, it relies on something that falls short of the value, instead of something beyond it" (291). Often, it works together with hyperbole. In this passage, for example, Douglas uses litotes and hyperbole in combination to insist on his record as a loyal Democrat. Initially, he makes his point by reciting this record, a recital followed first by a litotes—"a pretty good Democrat"—an understatement apparently in marked contrast to that record. Then, indignant at so low an estimate of his services on the part of the newspaper, Douglas refers hyperbolically to his efforts on behalf of his party—"when I was exerting every nerve and every energy for James Buchanan [,the presidential candidate]." This hyperbole is followed by a repetition of the litotes—"a pretty good Democrat." In its first appearance, this understatement serves Douglas's argument by reinforcing the fact that he has consistently been an excellent Democrat. In its second appearance, after the hyperbole and at the emphatic end of a sentence, the litotes serves his argument by reinforcing a value, that of his contribution to his party. Litotes enables Douglas to insist on the quality of his record, while avoidng self-praise.

Irony. While hyperbole and litotes involve movement along a scale, irony involves a 180 degree turn: a meaning is expressed in opposition to the one apparently intended. Our example is from Lincoln's reply to Douglas in their first debate at Ottawa. Lincoln is responding to a speech in which, as a prelude to attacking him and his views, Douglas called him "a poor, simple, amiable, intelligent gentleman":

> And thereupon the judge [Douglas] instantly began arguing in favor of popular sovereignty, the right of the people to have slaves if they wanted them,

> and to exclude slavery if they wanted to do so. But, said a senator from Ohio, by the name of Chase, we more than suspect you do not mean that the people shall have the right to exclude slavery if they want to, and if you do mean it, accept an amendment expressly authorizing the people to exclude slavery. I believe that I have the amendment before me:
>
> "The people of the territory, through their appropriate representatives, may, if they see fit, prohibit the existence of slavery therein."
>
> I now state it as a fact to be taken back if there is any mistake in it, that Judge Douglas and those acting with him voted that amendment down. I now think that those that voted that down had a real reason for doing so. It looks to us since we have seen the Dred Scott decision come, holding that under the constitution the people cannot exclude slavery, it looks to outsiders, *poor, simple, amiable, intelligent gentlemen,* it looks as if it was the place left to put that Dred Scott decision in and now I say again that if there was another and a different reason other than the conclusion that I have drawn, it will avail the judge much more to point out to these people what the good reason was for voting that amendment down, rather than swelling himself and asserting that he may be provoked to call somebody a liar. (Lincoln-Douglas 70)

To Perelman and Olbrechts-Tyteca, irony not only serves an argumentative purpose, but is itself an indirect argument (207–208; 330). In Lincoln's irony we have an instance of this dual effect, triggered in each case by the incongruity that results from literal interpretation: Douglas and his pro-slavery cohorts, Lincoln wants us to infer, are mistaken if they think that knowledgeable voters cannot see through their machinations to the truth beneath. But this irony is also part of Lincoln's general argumentative purpose: His irony also implies that no knowledgeable voter would trust Douglas once they have seen through his machinations.

Tropes of Comparison

Metaphor. Metaphor is a form of comparison.[2] Our example comes from Douglas's opening speech at the Jonesboro debate. Douglas is comparing the differences between the North and South to the differences between two nations at war:

> There you have Mr. Lincoln's main proposition, upon which he bases his claim, stated in his own language. He tells you that this Republic cannot endure permanently divided into slave and free States, as our fathers made it. He says that they must all become free or all become slave; must be all one thing, or all the other, or this government cannot last. Why can't it last, if we will execute the government in the spirit and on the same principles

> upon which it was made? Mr. Lincoln by that proposition tells the South, "If you desire to maintain your institutions as they now are, you must not be satisfied with minding your own business, but you must *invade* Illinois and all other Northern States, and establish slavery here and make it universal." Then he tells the North, "You must not be satisfied with regulating your own affairs, and minding your own business, but if you desire to maintain your freedom, you must *invade* the Southern States and abolish slavery everywhere, in order to have them all the one thing or all the other." I say that these propositions are the inevitable and irresistible result of Mr. Lincoln's argument, inviting a *warfare between the North and South, to be carried out with ruthless vengeance*. All the one section or all the other shall be driven to the wall and reduced as a victim to the rapacity of the other. *What good can be done by this system of warfare?* Suppose the North was to succeed in *conquering* the South, who will be the gainer? Suppose the South should succeed in *conquering* the North, can the Union be preserved in that way? And why is this sectional *warfare* to be carried on between Northern and Southern States till there shall be uniformity in all the institutions of the State? Because Mr. Lincoln says that "a house divided against itself cannot stand," and pretends that this scripture quotation, using language of the Lord himself, is applicable to the American Union and the American Constitution. (Lincoln-Douglas 149)

Perelman and Olbrechts-Tyteca devote special attention to metaphor, which they consider a condensed analogy, one that operates by interpreting the *theme*, the subject-matter of the metaphor, in terms of the *phoros*, the subject-matter to which the theme is being compared. For example, if we interpret the theme of the life cycle in terms of the phoros of the day cycle, we derive the metaphor, Old age is the evening of life:

THEME	PHOROS
A. Old Age	C. Evening
B. Life cycle	D. Day cycle

A is to *B* as *C* is to *D*.

In 1858, when Douglas made his speech, the comparison between North-South differences and warfare was just a way of speaking, a condensed analogy that can be represented as follows:

THEME	PHOROS
A. Differences	C. Warfare
B. Contending states	D. Contending nations

A is to *B* as *C* is to *D*.

To Perelman and Olbrechts-Tyteca, speakers make metaphor an element of argument by controlling the degree of fusion between theme and phoros, the degree to which a metaphor becomes an assertion of fact (400; 402; see also 378 and 381). In this passage, Douglas promotes the translation of metaphor into fact by integrating warfare into the grammar of his text: It appears as a noun ("warfare"), as a verb ("invade"), as an adjective ("conquering"), and as a prepositional phrase ("with ruthless vengeance"). Douglas also increases the likelihood of this fusion by his tacit reliance on a metaphoric commonplace: Argument is like war. This is a dead metaphor, one used routinely in such expressions as: He attacked his opponent, He defended his position. Douglas revivifies this dead metaphor; in so doing he gives it a strength that draws "on a stock of analogical material that gains ready acceptance because it is not merely known, but is integrated by language into the cultural tradition" (405). To the extent that this fusion succeeds, significance is transferred from phoros to theme: to believe in Douglas's metaphor is to believe in and be repelled by the dire consequences of the dilemma Lincoln poses. It is to turn metaphor into argument.

Personification. Personification is a special kind of metaphor, one in which an object or idea is likened to a human being. If I say that unscrupulous fishermen are *ravaging* the world's oceans, I am saying that these oceans are like a person who can be ravaged:

THEME	PHOROS
A. Harming	C. Ravaging
B. Oceans	D. Persons

A is to *B* as *C* is to *D*.

In his Jonesboro opening, in the passage just cited, Douglas uses personification as well as metaphor; he says: "*All the one section or all the other shall be driven to the wall and reduced as a victim to the rapacity of the other*" (lines 14–16). In this sentence, Douglas personifies the North and South by comparing them to human victims. In so doing, he uses personification in just the way Perelman and Olbrechts-Tyteca specify: "to stabilize the boundaries of a group and to give it coherence" (331). In the passage, metaphor and its sibling, personification, work together to help make Douglas's argumentative point that Lincoln's policies are dangerous to the country because they lead inevitably to violence and violation.

Tropes of Substitution

Metonymy and Synecdoche. The tradition does not clearly differentiate these two figures, which, together, cover substitutions of part for whole (as in "hands" for helpers); genus for species (as in "mortals" for "men"); species for genus (as in "bread" for "food"); and matter for object (as in "silver" for "money"). Among this class of substitutions there is a real connection; it is a characteristic of helpers that they have hands, of men that they are mortal, of bread that it is a food, and of money that it can be composed of silver. But also covered under the rubric of metonymy and synecdoche are substitutions that are attributive or symbolic—substitutions such as "crown" for "royalty," "mitre" for "bishop," or "White House" for "the presidency." In these cases, "the symbol and the thing symbolized are integrated into a mythical or speculative reality in which they are mutual participants" (*The New Rhetoric* 332). Substitutions of the first kind tend to be culturally invariant; those of the second, culturally relative. Nevertheless, those of the second can be very powerful in particular cultures; as with the American flag, they can evoke a whole way of life. While the tradition does not clearly differentiate between synecdoche and metonomy, Perelman and Olbrechts-Tyteca do. They assign to the former those connections that are real, and to the latter those that are symbolic (331–337). We will follow their practice.

Using the Belgians' terminology, Lincoln is employing synecdoche when, in a letter of condolence to Mrs. Bixby he writes:

> I have been shown in the files of the war Department a statement of the Adjutant General of Massachusetts, that you are the mother of five sons who have died gloriously on the fields of battle.
>
> I feel how weak and fruitless must be any word of mine which should attempt to beguile you from the grief of a loss so overwhelming. But I cannot refrain from tendering to you the consolation that may be found in the thanks of *the Republic* they died to save. (Lincoln 766)

Equally, he is using synecdoche in Perelman and Olbrechts-Tyteca's sense when, in a letter to Horace Greeley, he says:

> I would save *the Union*. I would save it the shortest way under the Constitution. The sooner the national authority can be restored, the nearer *the Union* will be "*the Union* as it was." If there be those who would not save *the Union*, unless they could at the same time save slavery, I do not agree with them. If there be those that would not save *the Union* unless they could at the same time destroy slavery, I do not agree with them. (Lincoln 652).

In both cases, Lincoln substitutes a characteristic of the United States for the name of this country; in each case, a different characteristic. Why? In the first case, Lincoln's argument depends on the public nature of the object of the sacrifice—a sacrifice for *res publica;* in the second case, his argument depends on the reason the war is being fought: to save the Union.

Again using Perelman and Olbrechts-Tyteca's distinction, Lincoln is employing metonymy when in a speech concerning the perpetuation of our political institutions he invokes the shade of Washington:

> They were the pillars of the temple of liberty; and now, that they have crumbled away, that temple must fall, unless we, their descendants, supply their places with other pillars, hewn from the solid quarry of sober reason. Passion has helped us; but it can do so no more. It will in future be our enemy. Reason, cold, calculating, unimpassioned reason, must furnish all the materials for our future support and defense.—Let those materials be moulded into general intelligence, sound morality, and, in particular, a reverence for the constitution and the laws: and that we improved to the last; that we remained free to the last; that we revered his name to the last; that, during his long sleep, we permitted no hostile foot to pass over or desecrate his resting place; shall be that which to learn the last trump shall awaken *OUR WASHINGTON*.[3] (Lincoln 84–85; emphasis omitted)

This is a case of metonymy because "OUR WASHINGTON" is a symbol for the perpetuation of our political institutions, the subject of Lincoln's speech. This metonymy serves Lincoln's argument: To be true to America is to be true to the memory of its founding father who will arise like Christ at the end of the world to judge the quality of our faith.

Ploce and polyptoton. In *ploce*, a word is repeated, though on its reappearance its meaning is altered (217). In his opening speech at Quincy, Lincoln uses this trope to make a point about Douglas's views on slavery:

> So I say again in regard to the arguments made when Judge Douglas says he don't care if slavery is voted up or voted down, whether he means it as an expression of sentiment, but only states it as a sort of view of the national policy, it is true to say it if he does not say that it is wrong, but if it be a wrong he cannot say that he would as soon see a wrong voted up as down. If Judge Douglas says that whatever community wants slaves has a right to have them, his logic is correct if he does not believe it a wrong. When he says that slave *property*, and horse and hog *property* ought to be allowed to go together to a territory upon principle, it is true if there is no difference between them, perhaps; but if one of them is right and the other wrong then there can be no equality between right and wrong. (Lincoln-Douglas 292–93)

While it is right to buy and sell hogs and horses, it is wrong, Lincoln says, to buy and sell slaves because, he implies, it is not part of the nature of human beings that they can be property. When Lincoln repeats the word, it becomes an evaluative term, a criticism of Douglas's values. What for Douglas are parallel, Lincoln says are for him contrasting expressions.

In polyptoton, the same word is also used more than once. But in polyptoton, in contrast to ploce, each repetition differs from its original occurrence in either case, number, or tense. In an address on the perpetuation of our political institutions, Lincoln speaks about a time when passion may have played a positive political role; he speaks of the feelings of hatred and revenge that motivated the colonists in their break from the British Empire, a moment in history during which even the basest of feelings could serve the just cause of political freedom: "But this state of feeling," he says, *must fade, is fading, has faded,* with the circumstances that produced it" (84). His polyptoton, his shift in tense—from the modal, to the progressive present, to the perfect—mirrors this change and, consequently, supports his argument that reason, not passion, must now be central in the preservation of our political institutions.

Schemes

Schemes cannot be defined by syntax alone. In anaphora, for example, we repeat the same word or phrase in successive clauses; we say, He did not know, he did not care, he did not help. What counts in classifying this scheme, however, is not only the fact of repetition, but also the parallels and contrasts in meaning among the repeated elements. Any adequate definition of this scheme must include both syntax and semantics; it is through the interplay of syntax and semantics that all schemes achieve their effect of emphasizing either likeness or difference among their elements.

Schemes Emphasizing Likeness

Anaphora and epistrophe. Anaphora and epistrophe are alike in that both figures highlight likeness in the phrases and clauses that they link. In the case of anaphora, initial words or phrases are repeated; in epistrophe, concluding words or phrases. In his reply to Lincoln at Quincy, Douglas uses anaphora when he says:

> Well, it may be that Republicans don't hold themselves bound by the laws of the land and the Constitution of the country, as expounded by the courts.

> It may be an article of the abolition creed that men who don't like a decision have a right to rebel against it. When [Lincoln] goes to preach that doctrine I think he will find some honest *Republicans*, some law-abiding men in that party who will repudiate such a monstrous doctrine as that. The decision in the Dred Scott case is binding on every American citizen alike, and yet Mr. Lincoln argues that *Republicans* are not bound by it because they are opposed to it. *Democrats* are bound by it because they don't resist it. *A Democrat* cannot resist the constituted authorities of his country. *A Democrat* is a law-abiding man. *A Democrat* stands by the Constitution, by the laws, by the constituted authorities, and relies upon liberty as protected by law, and not upon mob or physical violence. (Lincoln-Douglas 305)

In the first five sentences of this passage, Douglas refers to the two groups of party members in the plural. In the last three sentences, he switches number: In anaphoric repetition, he repeatedly refers to Democratic party members in the singular, each sentence equating party membership and obedience to the law of the land. The shift from plural to singular exemplifies Perelman and Olbrechts-Tyteca's point that "the use of the singular instead of the plural . . . has an undeniable import. We find in this substitution both an impression of presence due to the change of the group into a person, and a unification of viewpoint, the impossibility of distinguishing between the good and the bad that follows from this transformation" (162).[4]

In the case of epistrophe, final words or phrases are repeated. In his opening speech at Quincy, Lincoln says:

> Also, at Galesburg, I said something in regard to those Springfield resolutions that Judge Douglas had attempted to use upon me at Ottawa. I commented at some length upon the fact that they were, as presented, not genuine. Judge Douglas in his reply to me, seemed to be somewhat exasperated. He said that he would never have believed that Abraham Lincoln, as he kindly called me, would have attempted such a thing as I had attempted on that occasion, and among other expressions that he used toward me was *that I had dared to say forgery—that I had dared to say forgery*! Well, yes, Judge, *I did dare say forgery*. But in this political canvass the Judge ought to remember *that I was not the first who dared to say forgery*. (Lincoln-Douglas 287)

In its progressive occurrences at the conclusion of each of a sequence of sentences, Lincoln's refrain alters significantly: in its first two occurrences, it is an indignant accusation; at the conclusion of the next sentence, with a change of tense, it becomes the mere affirmation of a historical truth; at the conclusion of the last, it becomes a vindication: Lincoln is merely defending himself against character assassination.

Lincoln's epistrophe depends for its effect on verbal likeness; but, as we move from repetition to repetition, that likeness serves only to make apparent significant differences. By means of the shifts in effect that epistrophe permits, Lincoln is able to support his claim that he had nothing to do with the radical Springfield resolutions, resolutions that called for the repeal of the fugitive slave law, the emancipation of slaves in the nation's capital, and other "Black Republican" goals. At the same time, through the insinuation of repetition, he is able to cast aspersions on Douglas's character as a man and a politician.

Polysyndeton and asyndeton. In asyndeton, expected conjunctions between words, phrases, and clauses are omitted; in polysyndeton, more conjunctions are used than seem necessary. First, we will exemply these two schemes; then we will attempt to explain their contrasting argumentative effects. In 1839, in the close of his speech against the administration's subtreasury scheme, Lincoln uses asyndeton when he says:

> Let none falter, who thinks he is right, and we may succeed. But if, after all, we shall fail, be it so.—We still have the proud consolation of saying to our consciences, and to the departed shade of our country's freedom, that the cause approved of our judgment, and adored of our hearts, *in disaster, in chains, in torture, in death,* we never faltered in defending. (Lincoln 112)

In the debate at Alton, Douglas uses polysyndeton when he accuses Lincoln of having supported neither the Mexican War nor the troops in the field:

> It is one thing to be opposed to the declaration of war, and another thing to take the side of the enemy against your own country, for the war was commenced and our army was in Mexico at the time. . . . they were surrounded by the dangers, *and* the guns, *and* the poison of the enemy, *and* then it was that Corwin made his speech, stating that American soldiers ought to be welcomed to hospitable graves with bloody hands, *and* Ashmun and Lincoln voted in the House that the war was unconstitutional and unjust, *and* Lincoln's vote was sent to Mexico, *and* read to the army to prove to the army of the Mexicans that there was a Mexican party in the Congress of the United States. (Lincoln-Douglas 364)

In his *Philosophy of Rhetoric*, George Campbell claims that both asyndeton and polysyndeton, both an excess and a paucity of connectives, can have a positive rhetorical effect. As a solution to this apparent paradox, he suggests that these effects are different: In the former case, "celerity of operation, and fervour of narration" are expressed; in the latter, there is "a deliberate attention to every circumstance, as being of importance" (368). In Campbell's terms, in this passage Lincoln, by his omission of an expected "and," is underlining his fervor in the anti-subtreasury cause; on the other hand, in the second passage, Douglas is using his "ands" to emphasize each of the many ways that Lincoln has been disloyal to his country while in its supposed service as its representative.

Schemes Emphasizing Difference

Antithesis. Antithesis uses syntactic structure to emphasize conceptual contrast. Our example comes from Lincoln's annual message to Congress in 1862, proposing a plan for the gradual compensated emancipation of slaves:

> We say we are for the Union. The world will not forget that we say this. We know how to save the Union. The world knows we do know how to save it. We—even we here—hold the power and bear the responsibility. *In giving freedom to the slave, we assure freedom to the free*—honorable alike in what we give, and what we preserve. *We shall nobly save, or meanly lose,* the last best hope of earth. *Other means may succeed; this could not fail.* The way is plain, peaceful, generous, just—a way in which, if followed, the world will forever applaud, and God must forever bless. (Lincoln 688)

Antithesis clearly crosses any strict line that assigns schemes to syntax and tropes to semantics. Lanham defines antithesis as "conjoining contrasting ideas"; Harris, as a figure that "establishes a clear, contrasting relationship between two ideas by joining them together or juxtaposing them, often in parallel structure"; Corbett, as "the juxtaposing of contrasting ideas, often in parallel structure" (429). Perelman and Olbrechts-Tyteca agree. Speaking of a particular kind of antithesis, one that involves the reversal of a pair of opposing terms, they say, "When the reversal is shown by the position of the words, it can assume the aspect of a figure" (428).

In this peroration, in accordance with these definitions, Lincoln's three antitheses employ both syntax and semantics to attain their effect. Lincoln furthers his argument through antithesis by linking the adoption of his plan to words of positive connotation, while linking its rejection to words that are negatively charged The syntactic and semantic juxtapositions—"slave-free," "nobly save-meanly lose," "succeed-fail"—dramatize the choice he has put before the Congress.

Figures of Communion

According to Perelman and Olbrechts-Tyteca, figures of communion achieve their effect "through [reference] to a common culture, tradition, or past"; they "[create] a feeling of confidence, by showing that the speaker and his audience have common values" (177; 496). Allusion and quotation will be our examples of figures of communion.

Allusion and Quotation. Allusion is an indirect reference to a text, object, or event of particular salience to the group addressed. As our example, we take the allusion to the Old Testament in Lincoln's 1842 address delivered before the Springfield Washington Temperance Society:

> There seems ever to have been a proneness in the brilliant, and warm-blooded to fall into this vice. The demon of intemperance ever seems to have delighted in sucking the blood of genius and of generosity. What one of us but can call to mind some dear relative, more promising in youth than all his fellows, who has fallen a sacrifice to his rapacity? He ever seems to have gone forth, like the Egyptian angel of death, commissioned to slay if not the first, the fairest born of every family. Shall he now be arrested in his desolating career? In that arrest, all can give aid that will; and who shall be excused that can, and will not? (Lincoln 139; emphasis omitted)

In this speech Lincoln pleads for compassion and persuasion rather than ostracism and condemnation as a cure for chronic drunkenness. To support his claim before an audience of professing Christians, he alludes to the passage in the Old Testament in which the Lord punishes the Egyptians for withholding freedom from the Hebrew nation:

> For I will pass through the land of Egypt this night, and will smite all the firstborn in the land of Egypt, both man and beast; and against all the gods of Egypt I will execute judgment: I am the LORD. And it came to pass, that at midnight the LORD smote all the firstborn in the land of Egypt, from the firstborn of Pharoah that sat on his throne unto the firstborn of the captive that was in the dungeon; and all the firstborn of cattle (Exodus 11:5 and 12:12)

Lincoln furthers his argumentative purpose by establishing communion with his audience, suggesting thereby that, in so far as they are fellow Christians, they should concur with his point of view in treating chronic drunkenness less as a moral flaw than as an unfortunate affliction.

Quotation can also serve the purposes of argument through communion, but only "when it is not fulfilling its normal role of backing up statement with the weight of authority" (*New Rhetoric* 177). Lincoln ends his early speech on "The Perpetuation of Our Political Institutions" as follows: "Upon these let the proud fabric of freedom rest, as the rock of its basis; and as truly has been said of the only greater institution, "*the gates of hell shall not prevail against it*" (Lincoln 85). This is a direct quotation from Matthew 16: 18; moreover, it is important to Lincoln that his audience recognize its exact New Testament context: So long as we maintain "*a reverence for the constitution and laws*" (Lincoln 84–85; Lincoln's emphasis), he says, the gates of hell shall not prevail against our democracy, any more than they did against the Church that Christ founded. The quotation supports Lincoln's argument by linking the fate of America to the fate of the religion of most of its inhabitants.

Patterns of Tropes and Schemes: Public Discourse, Philosophy, and Science

We would now like to shift our object of study; to demonstrate the pervasiveness of figures as a component of arguments, we would now like to show how *patterns* of figures function in arguments in public address, in philosophy and science. Let us start on familiar ground—Lincoln's Gettysburg Address:

> Four score and seven years ago our fathers brought forth upon this continent, a new nation, conceived in Liberty, and dedicated to the proposition that all men are created equal.
>
> Now we are engaged in a great civil war, testing whether that nation, or any nation so conceived and so dedicated, can long endure. We are met on a great battle-field of that war. We have come to dedicate a portion of that field, as a final resting-place for those who gave their lives that this nation might live. It is altogether fitting and proper that we should do this.
>
> But in a larger sense, we cannot dedicate—we cannot consecrate—we cannot hallow—this ground. The brave men, living and dead, who struggled here, have consecrated it, far above our poor power to add or detract. The world will little note, nor long remember what we say here, but it can never forget what they did here. It is for us the living, rather, to be dedicated here to the unfinished work which they who fought here have thus far so nobly advanced. It is rather for us to be here dedicated to the great task remaining before us—that from these honored dead we take increased devo-

> tion to that cause for which they gave the last full measure of devotion—that we here highly resolve that these dead shall not have died in vain—that this nation, under God, shall have a new birth of freedom—and that government of the people, for the people, by the people, shall not perish from the earth. (Lincoln 734)

In his first two paragraphs, Lincoln tells the story of the battle of Gettysburg as a continuation of the act of founding the nation. In this narrative, he represents that nation metaphorically as a living being, born in Liberty, in danger now of being torn apart by civil war. The metaphor is deepened and extended in the phrase, "who gave their lives that this nation might live." Here Lincoln combines personification with polyptoton to link the soldiers' death directly to the preservation of the living Union. By the end of the speech, Lincoln has virtually fused the theme of the survival of the nation to the phoros of the survival of a living being; in the phrases "new birth of freedom" and "shall not perish from the earth," he reiterates his central metaphor; in the phrase, "government of the people, for the people, by the people" (16), he makes the nation literally its people. We see here demonstrated Perelman and Olbrechts-Tyteca's insight that "fusion of the terms of theme and phoros, bringing their respective spheres closer together, makes it easier to obtain argumentative effects" (400).

In philosophy also patterns of metaphor achieve argumentative effects. At the center of Descartes's *First Meditation* lies a dead metaphor to which he gives renewed existence: Life is a dream. The *First Meditation* thus exemplifies Perelman and Olbrechts-Tyteca's insight that "a stereotyped metaphorical expression can come to life again in the mouth of certain speakers, because it is presumed that, when they use it, it cannot have its usual meaning. Poets and philosophers are perhaps privileged in this respect" (407). In Descartes's hands, this dead metaphor, life is a dream, comes alive in two ways. In its first appearance, it recreates a mental state that may foreclose the possibility of certain knowledge:

> How often, asleep at night, am I convinced . . . that I am here in my dressing-gown, sitting by the fire—when in fact I am lying undressed in bed! Yet at the moment my eyes are certainly wide awake when I look at this piece of paper; I shake my head and it is not asleep; as I stretch out and feel my hand I do so deliberately, and I know what I am doing. All this would not happen with such distinctness to someone asleep. Indeed! As if I did not remember other occasions when I have been tricked by exactly similar thoughts while asleep! As I think about this more carefully, I see plainly that

> there are never any sure signs by means of which being awake can be distinguished from being asleep. The result is that I begin to feel dazed, and this feeling only reinforces the notion that I may be asleep. (Dicker 10)

In the wake of the possibility that the world we experience may be a total deception, the dream metaphor surfaces again, this time making vivid the temptation to abandon the pursuit of truth:

> I am like a prisoner who is enjoying an imaginary freedom while asleep; while he begins to suspect that he is asleep, he dreads being woken up, and goes along with the pleasant illusion as long as he can. In the same way, I happily slide back into my old opinions and dread being shaken out of them, for fear that my peaceful sleep may be followed by hard labour when I wake, and that I shall have to toil, not in the light, but amid the inextricable darkness of the problems I have now raised. (Dicker 12)

Descartes's *First Meditation* also exemplifies Perelman and Olbrechts-Tyteca's observation that the "multiple analogies can support each other" (392). In this passage, it is in interaction with analogies to prisoners and to light that the dream analogy reinforces the difficulty in maintaining our optimism in the face of the intellectual and spiritual difficulties that must accompany our search for the truth. With Descartes's *First Meditation* before us, it is easy to see the justice of the Belgians' observation that "it is not surprising that metaphor, with its fusion of spheres and transcendence of traditional classifications, should be, par excellence, the tool of poetic and philosophical creation" (404).

And of scientific creation as well. According to the Belgians, science transforms into facts and laws the analogies that are at the heart of metaphor: "as a link in the chain of inductive reasoning," Perelman and Olbrechts-Tyteca say, "analogy finds a place in science, where it serves rather as a means of invention than as a means of proof. If the analogy is a fruitful one, theme and phoros are transformed into examples or illustrations of a more general law, and by their relation to this law there is a unification of the fields of the theme and the phoros" (396).

The discovery of the genetic code exemplifies Perelman and Olbrechts-Tyteca's thesis. In 1944 in *What is Life?* the famous physicist Erwin Schrödinger hypothesized that "with the molecular picture of the gene it is no longer inconceivable that [a] miniature code should precisely correspond with a highly complicated and specified plan of development and should somehow contain the means to put it in operation" (66). The analogy is between genetic influence and a code.

In 1953, James Watson and Francis Crick discovered that DNA, the genetic substance, contained only four bases—adenine (A), thymine (T), guanine (G), cytosine (C)—arranged in the form of a double helix. This suggested that genetic transfer might occur when the helices unwound, each serving as a template, a "copying mechanism" (738) for this transfer. It soon transpired that it was not DNA, but closely related RNA, that was central to the elucidation of the "code." Its four "letters" were G, C, A, U (for uracil, a substitute for thymine). Crick and his associates noticed that, if these were combined into "words" three letters long, an arrangement was possible in which a correct reading would be independent of starting place. Such a code would be "comma free"; that is, the genetic "language" would be free of stop and start signals. This code prohibited certain combinations of letters, among them, the combination UUU (1953).

But in 1961 Marshall Nirenberg and J. Heinrich Matthaei established by experimental means that the combination UUU existed in nature; therefore, the code had to have start and stop signals; it had to have punctuation. Both Crick and Nirenberg had used the same analogy, a fruitful analogy for both. But the analogy that gave Nirenberg the correct answer led Crick astray. This is entirely in accord with Perelman and Olbrechts-Tyteca's views (Gross 28–30).

Crick's reception of the bad news that his hypothesis was incorrect conforms to the Belgians' claim that, once scientific facts and laws are established, metaphor in science disappears from view.[5] Hearing about Nirenberg and Matthaei's devastating critique of his comma-free system at a Biochemical Congress in Moscow, Crick wrote:

> The audience of Symposium [One] was startled by the announcement of Nirenberg that he and Matthaei had produced polypheylalanine (that is, a polypeptide all the residues of which are phenylalanine) by adding polyuridylic acid (that is, an RNA the bases of which are all uracil) to a cell-free system which can synthesize protein. This implies that a sequence of uracils codes for phenylalanine. (Crick et al. 1961, p. 1232)

This discovery forced Crick to reject his comma-free formulation in favor of the alternate hypothesis that "the correct choice [is] made by starting at a fixed point along the sequence of bases three (or four, or whatever) at a time." Such ready agreement demonstrates not so much fellow-feeling as necessary assent to verification based on agreed-upon procedures (Gross 31).

Conclusion and Limitations

It is a strength of Perelman and Olbrechts-Tyteca that they insist on an argumentative role for figures in public address, philosophy, and science. But while they can explain how a particular figure functions in the argument of which it is a part, they cannot explain why that particular figure was chosen over its possible rivals. Nor can we. There is an additional problem. Perelman and Olbrechts-Tyteca offer us almost no guidance in grappling with our intuition that the figures also have a role in emotional proofs. They are aware of the problem; they refer in passing to the part played by schemes in creating persuasive emotional effects (456). But they do not pursue this point. Their almost complete neglect of emotion may be an effect of a tacit conviction, almost a commonplace among those firmly within the Enlightenment tradition, that the rational and the emotional are directly opposed.

CHAPTER 10

Presence as Synergy

We end this book with a chapter on presence, a fitting conclusion, we think, since presence in its most interesting form is not the isolated effect of the elements of arrangement, style, and invention, but the cumulative effect of interactions among these. This form of presence has as its object not the alteration or reinforcement of isolated attitudes or beliefs, but of fundamental principles: the real in the social and material universe and the significant in the realm of values. Presence of this sort is a superordinate concept, a second-order effect that relies on a synergy of first-order effects—those achieved, one by one, at the level of invention, arrangement, and style. In this chapter, we will define superordinate presence; then, to illustrate its scope, we will show it at work in three forms of discourse: public address, philosophy, and science. We will then address a problem that has troubled one of the most astute of Perelman and Olbrechts-Tyteca's commentators; namely, that presence seems inconsistent with the Belgians' philosophy of argumentation, a philosophy with reason at its center. Finally, we will offer a critique of their view that rhetorical presence is a technical concept only, without any existential implications.

Defining Presence

Presence is a consequence of the need of rhetoricians to select from a mass of material and a variety of rhetorical means what they will actually present to an audience. When they make this selection with an eye to persuading particular audiences, they are using presence methodologically: they are taking advantage of the fact that "the thing on which the eye dwells, that which is best or most often seen is, by that very circumstance, overestimated" (Perelman and Olbrechts-Tyteca 116–117). The effect of presence is initially psychological: "to [fill] the whole field of consciousness" (118). But such is the nature of communication that what is "at first a psychological phenomenon, becomes an essential element in argumentation" (117). In this section we define presence and illustrate its use as an element in argumentation.

Presence has its antecedents. In the third book of his *Rhetoric*, Aristotle distinguishes between metaphors with and metaphors without *energeia*. If you call a good man "four-square," you are using the latter sort of metaphor; if you say that an arrow is "eager to fly," you are using the former sort (3.11.1). For Aristotle, metaphor with energeia brings an inanimate object to life; in Perelman and Olbrechts-Tyteca's terminology, the impending flight of the arrow has a presence that the man has not, a presence that is the consequence of a rhetorical technique, a deliberate choice of one form of expression over another. Initially, the effect is psychological; the personification of the arrow draws the listener's attention to its flight. But, the Belgians also say, these techniques of presence can have a persuasive role; that is, they can play a part in increasing or decreasing adherence to beliefs. For example, when Lincoln compares the number of hanged men with the abundance of Spanish moss hanging from the trees, as in the last chapter, he is increasing their presence in the interest of condemning mob violence.

Perelman and Olbrechts-Tyteca freely acknowledge that this view has been anticipated by the 18th-century rhetorical theorist, George Campbell (118). Campbell calls his anticipations of presence "circumstances in the object presented by the speaker which serve to awaken and inflame the passions of the hearers" (90), for him an essential ingredient in persuasion. Campbell inventories these circumstances: the plausibility of the event, its importance to the auditors, its closeness in space and time, the closeness of the relation between the auditors and the persons involved, and the degree of auditor interest in the event's consequences. These circumstances operate in concert, as his example from Cicero shows (90–93). In his attack on Verres, who as a provincial administrator has crucified a Roman citizen, Messana, Cicero says:

> How must we be affected now, when we hear of the anguish of our own kinsman? I say our kinsman, for we must recognize blood-kinship between all Roman citizens; truth, not less than concern for the general safety, bids us do so. And now in this place all the citizens of Rome, all those who are here and all who are elsewhere, are looking to you to do strict justice, appealing to your honour, imploring your help. They believe that their every right and

> interest and advantage, yes, that the whole of their liberty, depends on the verdict that you give. (659)

In this passage, Cicero appeals simultaneously to the closeness of the victim to the auditors, their "kinsman," to the "here and now" of the offense, and to the interest of Roman citizens in protecting their rights anywhere Rome has sovereignty. It is these factors operating in concert that give the event its rhetorical presence.

To these circumstances, we must add a quality of style Campbell calls vivacity, a quality "adapted to please the imagination, and consequently to fix the attention" (285). It depends on "the choice of words, their number, and their arrangement" (285). Perelman and Olbrechts-Tyteca clearly have such vivacity in mind when they speak of such figures of speech as *interpretatio*, "the explanation of one expression by another, not so much for purposes of clarification, as to increase the feeling of presence: 'It is the republic you have completely upset, the state you have completely destroyed'"(176; see also 167, 174–77, 236, 240, 331). To style and circumstances, Perelman and Olbrechts-Tyteca add arrangement as a device for conferring presence: "the order of the arguments will . . . be dictated in [some] measure by the desire . . . to confer presence on certain elements" (492).

These are first-order effects. When we say that the metaphor, The arrow is eager to fly, makes its impending flight present to listeners, we speak of the effect of an isolated stylistic element. But presence is not merely an isolated phenomenon; the various instances of presence in a text can also form patterns whose effect is synergistic. In its synergistic guise, presence is a general rhetorical strategy, a second-order effect whose purpose Louise Karon nicely captures when she says that through presence, "*we establish the real. The real* is as much a hypothetical construct as is the universal audience" (169). This is not a vapid metaphysical statement but a precise observation about the reach of this rhetorical strategy: "The values accepted by the audience, the speaker's prestige, and the very language he uses, all these elements are in constant interaction when one wishes to gain the adherence of minds" (132). Perelman and Olbrechts-Tyteca's presence can be extended from a first to a second-order effect, one that is global in nature; presence can encompass the whole of the speech. We will call this superordinate presence.

Rhetorical critics have endorsed the utility of superordinate presence by demonstrating how individual instances of the first-order effect can coalesce to form patterns whose effects are simultaneously psychological and argumentative. In his study of presence in Al Gore's rhetoric, John Murphy deals with the interaction of analogies in an environmental polemic; in their study of presence in nuclear rhetoric, Charles Kauffman and Donn Parson address patterns of metaphor in the debate over nuclear defense; in his study of presence in science, Alan Gross discusses patterns of style and arrangement in texts from avian taxonomy. These analyses conform to Karon's interpretation of presence as "created chiefly through techniques of style, delivery, and disposition [arrangement]" (164). In each case this creation also serves the purposes of argument.

Kaufmann and Parson make the additional important point, anticipated by Perelman and Olbrechts-Tyteca (118), that the suppression of presence can have a persuasive effect. They show that metaphors with and without *energeia* can be used systematically, on the one hand, to alarm, and on the other, to dampen, public anxieties. For example, using metaphors with *energeia*, President Reagan speaks of "antique" Titan missiles that leave the United States "naked" to attack; he depicts the Soviet Union as an "Evil Empire" led by "monsters." On the other hand, using metaphors without *energeia*, General Gordon Fornell creates an antipresence designed to sidestep public anxiety in the interest of further weapons procurement: "The current Soviet ICBM force of 1,398 missiles, of which over 800 are SS-17, SS-18, and SS-19 ICBMs, represents *a dangerous countermilitary asymmetry which must be corrected in the near term*" (99–100; emphasis mine). The systematic use of such colorless metaphors increases adherence by dampening what might otherwise be legitimate anxieties.

It is in the spirit of this more global view of presence that we will analyze the extended passages below, from political oratory, from philosophy, and from science.

Presence in Political Oratory

A passage from Stephen Douglas's reply to Lincoln in the second of the Lincoln-Douglas debates at Freeport, Illinois, on August 27, 1858, will provide us with an example of the way in which individual rhetorical devices work together to produce a second-order global effect in political oratory. We will show that in their synergy they create an alternate reality, a world in which Abraham Lincoln ought to be defeated for the Senate for the very good reason that his stubborn defense of black rights stands in the way of America's progress. In pursuing our goal, we must, given the nature of our task, cite fairly lengthy passages; we beg the reader's indulgence in coping with the difficulties inherent in connecting such lengthy passages to their surrounding text:

> The fourth question [of Mr. Lincoln] is, Are you in favor of acquiring more territory, without regard to how it may affect the country on the slavery question? The question is very ingeniously and cunningly put. The Black Republican party, in their creed, laid down the proposition that under no circumstances would we acquire any more territory, unless slavery be first prohibited in the country. I ask Mr. Lincoln whether he is in favor of the proposition. Are you against any further acquisition of territory under any circumstances, unless slavery is prohibited? That he didn't like to answer. I ask him if he stands up to that article in the platform, and he turns around, Yankee fashion, and without answering it himself, asks me: Are you opposed to admitting a slave Territory? I answer him that, whenever it becomes necessary for our growth and progress to acquire more territory, I am for it without reference to the question of slavery, and when we have got it, that we leave the people in the Territory free to do as they please—either to make a slave Territory or a free Territory, just as they choose. (Lincoln-Douglas 109)

In this section of his speech, Douglas increases the presence of this passage by creating a fictional debate between Lincoln and himself, cast in the present tense (Perelman and Olbrechts-Tyteca 160–61). In this mock debate, Lincoln is placed center-stage, but only as a ventriloquist's dummy: While he is actually present, sharing the stage with Douglas, he is sworn to silence as part of the etiquette of debate. Douglas takes advantage of this enforced silence by depicting a fictional Lincoln, a pawn of the "black" Republicans, and a waffler on the issues.

In the next section of his speech, Douglas shifts from popular sovereignty to territorial expansion, a necessity whose untroubled progress popular sovereignty will guarantee:

> It is idle to tell me, and to tell you, that we have territory enough now. Our fathers supposed that we had enough when we acquired the territory only to the Mississippi River; but in view of the growth and expansion of the country, we were satisfied that we needed more territory, and we acquired the Louisiana Territory, including the west bank of the Mississippi River to the British Possessions. Then we acquired Oregon, and then California and New Mexico. We have enough now for the present, but this is a young nation and a growing nation. It swarms as often as a bee hive, turning out a new swarm every year, and they must have new hives in which they may gather and make their honey. In less than fifteen years the same ratio of progress that has distinguished this country for the last fifteen years, would occupy every vacant foot of land between this and the Pacific Ocean under

> the government of the United States and will you not continue to increase after that time as well as now? I tell you to increase, to multiply, to expand, is the law of this nation's existence. You cannot limit this great country by mere boundary lines, saying thus far thou must go and no further. Any one of you, gentlemen, might as well say to his son, twelve years of age: "You are now big enough; you mustn't grow any larger," and, in order to prevent growth, put a hoop around him to keep him to his present size. So with this great nation. With our national increase going on with a rapidity unknown in any other part of the globe—with a tide of immigration that is fleeing from despotism in the Old World, and seeking refuge in our own—there is a constant pouring into this country that requires more land, more territory on which to settle, and just as fast as our interests, our destinies and our necessities require additional territory—in the South or in the North, or in the islands of the Ocean—I am for it. And when we get it I will leave the people of each Territory free, according to the Nebraska Bill, to do as they please on the subject of slavery and every other question. (Lincoln-Douglas 109–110)

In this section of his speech, Douglas shifts from the affirmation of popular sovereignty to its motivating force: the need to acquire new territory without respect to the divisive issue of slavery. He emphasizes the inevitability of this expansion by means of metaphors, by viewing the *theme* of political growth in terms of the *phoros* of natural growth: America must grow as bees swarm from the hive, as children grow to be adults, as the tide rolls in. Political expansion is even linked by allusion to God's command "to increase, to multiply" in a land as conveniently "vacant" as was the earth to Adam and Eve. These inevitable links are supported by schemes, by the repeated use of epistrophe: "there is a constant pouring into this country that requires more land, more territory on which to settle, and just as fast as our interests, our destinies and our necessities require additional territory—in the South or in the North, or in the islands of the Ocean."

Epistrophe increases the presence of the passage by permitting, even encouraging, the leap from syntax to significance. This is because syntactic parallelism implies semantic common ground: if I am taking my bat, my ball, and my glove to the field, I am taking my *baseball equipment* to the field. Analogously, "more land, more territory" implies that political organization naturally follows physical occupation; "our interests, our destinies and our necessities" implies that this sovereign expansion is a matter of fate; "in the South or in the North or in the islands of the Ocean" implies that imperial expansion is a natural extension of legitimate Continental claims.

In his last sentence, Douglas changes rhetorical tactics. He offers us, not a rhetorical flourish, but only his bald conclusion that "when we get it I will leave the people of each territory free, according to the Nebraska Bill, to do as they please on the subject of slavery and every other question." This is an instance of the use of syntax in the interest of the suppression of presence. In addition, the syntactic parallelism at the end of Douglas's sentence implies that slavery is just another political question, not, as Lincoln asserts, the most important political question.

In the final section of his speech with which we will deal, Douglas turns to Lincoln himself, his real polemical target:

> I trust now that Mr. Lincoln will deem himself answered on these few points. He racked his brain so much in devising these few questions that he exhausted himself, and had not the strength enough left to invent another but as soon as he can hold a council of his advisors, by getting Lovejoy, and Farnsworth and Giddings and Fred. Douglass together, he will then frame and propound the other interrogator[ies]. I have no doubt you think they are all good men—good Black Republicans. Fred. Douglass is a very good man. The last time I came here to make a speech, while I was talking on the stand to you people of Freeport, as I am today, I saw a carriage, and a magnificent one too, drive up and take its position on the outside of the crowd, with a beautiful young lady on the front seat, with a man and Fred. Douglass, the negro, on the back seat, and the owner of the carriage in front driving the negro. I witnessed that here in your town.
>
> A VOICE—What of it?
>
> JUDGE DOUGLAS—What of it! All I have to say is this, if you Black Republicans think that the negro ought to be on a social equality with young wives and daughters, and ride in the carriage with the wife while the master of the carriage drives the team, you have a perfect right to do so. I am told also that one of Fred. Douglass' kinsmen, another rich black negro, is now traveling this part of the State making speeches for his friend Mr. Lincoln, who is the champion of the black man's party. All I have got to say on that subject is this, those of you who believe that the nigger is your equal, and ought to be on an equality with you socially, politically and legally, have a right to entertain those opinions, and of course will vote for Mr. Lincoln. (Lincoln-Douglas 110–111)

In this speech, by means of *ploce*, by repeating the adjective "good" three times with three different significations, the last two ironic, Douglas prepares the way for an anecdote designed to exemplify the unfortunate racial consequences of Lincoln's policies. Douglas does not draw a moral from his tale, but a question from the crowd, apparently fortuitous, creates an opportunity on which he seizes. In his opinion, that party, and its representative, Mr. Lincoln, shift effortlessly from the equality of African-Americans as human beings who ought not to be enslaved (Lincoln's actual position) to their full equality "socially, politically, and legally" (a position from which Lincoln always distances himself). In the last sentence, the parenthetical "of course" provides the stylistic *coup de grâce:* A vote for Lincoln is a vote in favor of the social chaos of racial mixing, a chaos to which Lincoln's territorial policies will inevitably lead.

In Douglas's speech, the various devices of first-order presence form patterns that create a cumulative, second-order effect, a superordinate presence. The mock debate with Lincoln, the use of natural growth as a trope for imperial growth, the persistent epistrophes, the use of ploce to underline the frightening point of the racial anecdote, the vivid anecdote itself—these isolated instances of first-order presence coalesce to create an image of an expanding America in which white supremacy is guaranteed, and a contrasting image of Lincoln who, by inhibiting territorial expansion and encouraging miscegenation, would undermine all that America stands for. Lincoln's policies, Douglas says, are endangering the future of the country; a vote for him is a vote against America. Douglas is not merely saying these things; by verbal magic alone, he is creating a world in which these things are unquestionably true.

Presence in Philosophy

Presence is not limited to political oratory. It occurs as well in philosophy and science, though in these two forms of discourse style, arrangement and invention are constrained by the need to obtain the assent of the universal audience; in such discourses, language must be treated, not as a creator of worlds, but as a window, transparent to the truth.

We will take as our philosophical example an extended passage from Descartes's *Discourse on Method,* also commented on by Perelman and Olbrechts-Tyteca (359–360). It is a passage in which the philosopher creates a presence that justifies his inference that "as far as all the opinions I had accepted hitherto were concerned, I could not do better than undertake once and for all to be rid of them in order to replace them afterward either by better ones, or even by the same, once I had adjusted them by the plumbline of reason" (*Discourse* 37). We will see from this passage how by means of the devices of first-order presence, Descartes creates a second-order reality in which the dictates of common sense must be overturned in the interest of his radical views.

To prepare the way, Descartes relates a personal anecdote whose burden is that the "I" of the *Discourse* is a man of action forced by circumstances to contemplate, rather than a contemplative man:

> I was, at that time, in Germany, whither the wars, which have not finished there, had called me, and as I was returning from the coronation of the Emperor to join the army, the onset of winter held me up in quarters in which, finding no company to distract me, and having, fortunately, no cares or passions to disturb me, I spent the whole day shut up in a room heated by an enclosed stove, where I had complete leisure to meditate on my own thoughts. (*Discourse* 35)

The contrast with the beginning of the *Meditations*, written in Latin for a learned audience, is instructive. Descartes goes over the same ground, but creates a presence that is specifically philosophical: "Some years ago I was struck by the large number of falsehoods that I had accepted as true in my childhood, and by the highly doubtful nature of the whole edifice that I had subsequently based on them. I realized that it was necessary, once in the course of my life, to demolish everything completely and start again right from the foundations if I wanted to establish anything at all in the sciences that was stable and likely to last" (Dicker 9).

In the *Discourse*, this realization cannot be assumed; it must be established by a series of instances that make vivid the rule that, in the quest for truth, the systematic activity of a unified consciousness is generally to be preferred to its more haphazard counterpart, the work of many minds: "Among [my thoughts,] one of the first I examined was that often there is less perfection in works composed of several separate pieces and made by different masters, than in those at which only one person has worked."

To support his claim Descartes adduces five analogies. In the first, a building designed by a single architect is inevitably more admirable:

> So it is that one sees that buildings undertaken and completed by a single architect are usually more beautiful and better ordered than those that several architects have tried to put into shape, and making use of old walls which were built for other purposes.

In the second of Descartes's analogies, the layout of a city by a single town planner is inevitably more perfect:

> So it is that these old cities which, originally only villages, have become, through the passage of time, great towns, are usually so badly proportioned in comparison with those orderly towns which an engineer designs at will on some plain that, although the buildings, taken separately, often display as

> much art as the planned towns or even more, nevertheless, seeing how they are placed, with a big one here, a small one there, and how they cause the streets to bend and to be at different levels, one has the impression that they are more the product of chance than that of a human will operating according to reason. And if one considers that there have nevertheless always been officials responsible for the supervision of private building and for making it serve as an ornament for the public, one will see how difficult it is, by adding only to the construction of others, to arrive at any great degree of perfection.

In the third analogy, Descartes asserts that a constitution framed by a single legislator is inevitably better ordered, as is the true religion, "the laws of which God alone has made":

> So I thought to myself that the people who were formerly half savages, and who became civilized only gradually, making their laws only in so far as the harm done by crimes and quarrels forced them to do so, could not be so well organized as those who, from the moment at which they came together in association, observed the basic laws of some wise legislator; just as it is indeed certain that the state of the true religion, the laws of which God alone has made, must be incomparably better ordered than all the others. And, to speak of human beings, I believe that, if Sparta greatly flourished in times past, it was not on account of the excellence of each of its laws taken individually, seeing that many were very strange and even contrary to good morals, but because, having been invented by one man only, they all tended towards the same end. (*Discourse* 35–36)

The first two analogies, from architecture and town-planning, use unproblematic examples that make present the rule that single masters working alone generally produce more perfect and unified work; the third, from politics and religion, generalizes this rule to include conceptual objects. No one is likely to object to the common-sense rule these analogies exemplify.

In the fourth and fifth analogies, however, Descartes shifts conceptual ground. In his fourth analogy, he asserts that the reasoning of a single man of sense is inevitably closer to the truth than a patchwork of the knowledge found in books.

> And so I thought that the knowledge we acquire in books, at least that based on reasoning which is only probable and for which there is no proof, being composed and enlarged little by little by the opinions of many different people, does not approach the truth as closely as the simple reasoning of a man of good sense concerning things which he meets.

In the fifth and last analogy, Descartes avers that those led by reason from birth inevitably have the advantage of those who obtain their learning at the hands of several masters:

> So, finally I thought that as we have all been children before being men, and that we have had to be governed for a long time by our appetites and our teachers, the ones being often in opposition to the others and neither perhaps always giving us the best advice, it is almost impossible that our judgments be as rational or as sound as they would have been if we had had the full use of our reason from the moment of our birth, and if we had never been guided by anything else. (*Discourse* 36)

In concert, these five analogies are designed to create a superordinate presence that shakes us out of our complacency; that renders intolerable the selves we currently have; that allows us, not merely to see, but to experience our lives as the haphazard and unreflective products of our educations and our upbringings. Descartes achieves this disorienting effect, this disconcerting superordinate presence, by exploiting the gap between a grammatical superstructure that treats all five analogies as parallel and a conceptual base, in which, between the first three analogies and the last two, there is a stubborn disjunction that can be bridged only by accepting the Cartesian invitation to radical philosophical reflection.

These final two analogies insist that the original rule be thoroughly reinterpreted, since in each new case the "master" is the reason itself and the "work," the self. The sources of disunity Descartes identifies are not what we would ordinarily classify as haphazard practices; they are the two chief sources of all adult selves, our education and our upbringing. It is these Descartes holds hostage to his methodological skepticism.

Presence in Science

Like philosophical presence, presence in science is restricted by its need to address a universal audience; as in philosophy, flamboyant exploitation of any sort is avoided. In our example, a paper on avian taxonomy, Fitzpatrick, and his co-workers, Willard, and Terborgh have discovered a new hummingbird in Peru. Their task is to describe it in such a way that their colleagues are convinced that this is indeed a new species. In pursuit of this goal, they use, not only the verbal means we have already talked about, but visual means as well. They are no purists; they are willing to use any appropriate verbal or visual means to bring this new species to life, to give it an indelible presence. They describe a species characterized by "a broad, pale buffy breast band [that] separates the smaller throat spots from larger and more numerous discs on the breast and flanks. In a few specimens the posterior border of the breast band is entirely defined by a broad row of these discs." They depict species behavior: "Initially a pair [of birds] was foraging around the walls of [a vine-covered sinkhole] and in the surrounding shrubs along the rim. Both male and female were observed perching on a rootlet, making frequent sallies to capture tiny flying insects." The use of these multiple perspectives is effective because it mimics the manner in which we confirm and make vivid our impressions of real physical objects: We see the rose, we smell it, we touch its petals. We know it is real.

To define the uniqueness of this new species, Fitzpatrick and his co-workers use pictures as well as words. The species is depicted by two very different means. In a full-color frontispiece, a male and female are displayed so as to show the species' typical feeding behavior; moreover, the dimorphic pair are so oriented that their species characteristics are fully in view. To supplement this frontispiece, Fitzpatrick and his co-workers create a black and white drawing that sets the new species beside its existing relatives in the manner of a police line-up: As a consequence, the distinctive combination of features that characterize the new species leap immediately into view. In this scientific article, the devices of first-order presence—the detailed descriptions of morphology and behavior, the illustration of the species in situ and in comparison with other, similar species—coalesce to create a superordinate presence that makes the new hummingbird real to science. Having given this new species a scientific presence, Fitzpatrick and his co-workers confirm its uniqueness by giving their discovery a name, *Heliangelus regalis*, Royal Sunangel, a name whose first element proclaims its resemblance to other species, and whose second proclaims its difference. As baptism makes a human being a member of the community of Christians, so this naming ceremony makes a hummingbird a member of the community of avian species known to science (paraphrased from Gross, 33–53).

Criticizing Presence

Our final task is to address a serious criticism of Perelmanian presence and to proffer a serious criticism of our own. We will address a criticism by Louise Karon—one that, while mistaken in our view, illuminates a central limitation of Perelman and Olbrechts-Tyteca's treatment of argument and argumentation. If their theory of argumentation is, as Karon rightly asserts, a generative theory of knowledge, and if presence is an inevitable element of argumentation, then, as Karon correctly infers, "presence will indeed be an equally important and inevitable component of [Perelman and Olbrechts-Tyteca's] theory of knowledge" (164). But, since their theory of knowledge has as its founding principle "the existence of a rational argumentation, an argumentation which, like Kant's categorical imperative, claims to be valid for the community of reasonable minds" (Perelman, *Idea* 97), this inclusion creates a problem: In the case of presence, "[the] strongest agents remain the imagination and the emotions" (Karon 165).

Karon thinks she has a solution to this problem: She feels that, since rational certitude leads to the cessation of doubt, a state in which conviction fills the consciousness, "conviction becomes the quintessence of presence" (175). This solution can hardly be correct, however, given Perelman and Olbrechts-Tyteca's own conviction that "only the existence of an argumentation that is neither compelling nor arbitrary can give meaning to human freedom, a state in which reasonable choice can be exercised" (514). The solution lies, rather, in understanding the equivocation inherent in Perelman and Olbrechts-Tyteca's project, an equivocation reflected in the subtitle of his major work: A Treatise on Argumentation. Is *The New Rhetoric* about the arguments people make, or about the process of argumentation? Is the book primarily about *arguments* or about *arguing*? The former, clearly; but it is Perelman's firm conviction that rational force lies, not in arguments themselves, but in their interaction, an interaction whose philosophical form is dialectic:

> In dialectical argumentation, it is conceptions considered as generally accepted that are confronted and contrasted with each other. Because of that, the dialectical method is the method *par excellence* of any philosophy which realizes the social, imperfect and incomplete aspect of philosophical knowledge, instead of relying upon intuitions and self-evident truths considered as irrefragable. (*Idea*, 167)

From this Perelmanian position, presence and, by inference, any element of argument, can be rationally redeemed only through argumentative interaction. Our example will be Lord Spencer's funeral eulogy for his sister, Diana, Princess of Wales. We will see that, simply by examining this eulogy, simply by analyzing the means by which Lord Spencer makes his late sister's virtuous character present to his audience, we cannot determine whether or not the presence he creates is rationally redeemed. This can be determined only by placing the eulogy in appropriate argumentative contexts: rationality is the by-product of the process of argument.

In our analysis, we will focus on the pattern of personal names, pronouns, and their predicates, devices of first-order presence that create, in the aggregate, a presence of a second order, a vivid image of Diana as a moral exemplar. The varying use of these devices corresponds with the arrangement of the speech, four culminating movements, in each of which the virtuous presence of Diana increases incrementally as a consequence of alterations in person and tense. In each movement, a new perspective is added. There is first an objective movement, characterized by the use of the pronoun with the past tense. Here is a typical example: "All over the world she was a symbol of selfless humanity." There is a second, addressive movement, in which Diana is spoken to in the second person and in the present tense, as if she were alive: "There is a temptation to rush to canonise your memory, there is no need to do so. You stand tall enough as a human being of unique qualities not to need to be seen as a saint." There is a third, personal movement in the third person and in the past tense, a movement in which Diana lives in the memory of those who love her and those whom she loved: "The last time I saw Diana was on July 1, her birthday in London, when typically she was not taking time to celebrate her special day with friends but was guest of honour at a special charity fundraising evening." Finally, there is a movement in which Diana is a presence in the future, despite her death: "We will not allow [William and Harry] to suffer the anguish that used regularly to drive you to tearful despair." As this pattern develops, Diana takes on more and more of the characteristics of a living person: someone who can still be addressed, someone still in the minds of loved ones, someone to whom the future still matters.

Diana's is not only a living but also an overwhelming moral presence. She is a caring human being, a good sister, and a good mother. Lord Spencer emphasizes these qualities directly and by contrast. Diana raises money for AIDS sufferers, and cares about "her beloved boys." But she is also mistreated by the royal family, who are, by implication, "simply immersed in duty and tradition" and the *paparazzi* who have made her "the most hunted person in the modern age." Diana is being praised at the expense of the press and royal family.

Lord Spencer has a warrant to speak on Diana's behalf because he loves his sister, that is, he loves the qualities that makes Diana a good sister, a good mother, and a good human being. To this there is a corollary, as Perelman and Olbrechts-Tyteca point out: "Irrespective of his wish or whether or not he himself uses connections of the act-person type, a speaker runs the risk that the hearer will regard him as intimately connected with his speech" (317). This is true without exception for epideictic oratory. Diana's presence as a moral exemplar is grounded in Lord Spencer's presence as a good brother, a good husband, and a good human being. The real moral presence in this speech, then, belongs to the speaker. It is Lord Spencer's moral presence, his love for Diana grounded in his love of her virtues, that entitles him to his anger at the press and at the royal family.

But it is, as it turns out, wrong for him to praise Diana at the expense of the royal family and the press. At issue is not the truth of Lord Spencer's statements; at issue, rather, is his right to make such statements, the authenticity of *his* moral presence. This is not an issue raised by the audience or by the rhetorical critic; it is an issue raised by Lord Spencer himself when eulogizing his sister: "the speaker's life, in so far as it is public, forms a long prelude to his speech," and, Perelman and Olbrechts-Tyteca might have added, a long postlude as well (317). Involved in a messy divorce in which his behavior toward his wife seems strikingly similar to Charles's alleged behavior to Diana, he is open to attack, not only as a wife abuser, but as a hypocrite: "Will somebody pinch me?" wrote Allison Pearson in Wednesday's *Evening Standard*. "Is this the same man who, at his sister's funeral just three months ago, lectured the Windsors on the loving conduct of family life? The same earl who implied that the souls of William and Harry would be safer in the embrace of the Spencers?"

We have here a powerful form of so-called *ad hominem* fallacy, in his case a perfectly good argument fully relevant to the issue at hand. Notice that neither Allison Pearson nor the *Evening Standard* has an independent moral authority. Their moral authority is entirely dependent on Lord Spencer's alleged hypocrisy. It is this authority that entitles them, not only to their criticism, but to their indignation. By praising Diana in the way that he did, Lord Spencer has opened himself to this particular line of attack. His portrait of Diana survives; her moral presence is redeemed rationally by the implicit consensus of the press. What does not survive, what is not rationally redeemed, is his right to praise his sister at the expense of the press and the royal family. Moreover, as a consequence of his loss of moral authority a new right is created, Allison Pearson's right to indignation that is rationally redeemed by that loss.

We need only note that this consensus is hardly stable; it is always and necessarily the creature of the process of argumentation, a process that creates and re-creates rational positions. The accusations against Lord Spencer may turn out to be groundless; it may transpire that Diana was less virtuous than she currently appears to the public and the press. This is entirely in accord with the fundamental tenet of Perelman and Olbrechts-Tyteca's philosophy of rhetoric: "Only the existence of an argumentation that is neither compelling nor arbitrary can give meaning to human freedom, a state in which reasonable choice can be exercised" (514).

We need to make one final point. While Perelman and Olbrechts-Tyteca give presence a central place in their theory of rhetoric, they specifically disavow its existential implications:

> This notion of presence, which we are speaking of here and which we consider to be of paramount importance for the technique of argumentation, is not a philosophical formulation. A philosophy that considers presence as a cornerstone of its structure—that of Buber or Sartre, for example—would connect it with an ontology or an anthropology. That is not our purpose. We are interested only in the technical aspect of the notion, which leads to the inevitable conclusion that all argumentation is selective. (119)

We are sympathetic with Perelman and Olbrechts-Tyteca's restraint, their desire to shun philosophical speculation of a certain sort; nevertheless we would like to suggest that, even in rhetorical theory, presence is more than a matter of technique; even within that theory presence has, despite their disavowal, existential implications.

We cannot demonstrate this claim in brief compass, a demonstration that in any case would be a long digression, given the purpose of this volume. Still, we can suggest a direction that the argument of this chapter opens up, one that leads away from presence viewed only as technique. Our text is a sonnet of Rainer Maria Rilke, "Archaic Torso of Apollo." This landmark of the modern German lyric is so deeply rooted in the nuances of its native language that no translation can preserve more than a whisper of its poetry. Fortunately, however, the poem may be paraphrased in a manner that preserves an insight central to our purposes:

> We did not know him when he was alive, when the eyes in that astounding head ripened like fruit. Still, even now his torso glows like a candelabra; though turned down low, his gaze penetrates steadily outward. If his stare did not do so, the surge of his breast would not dazzle you, nor would you see how his loins curve like a smile downward, flowing toward their generative center; if his stare did not do so, this stone would seem ill-formed and inert under his shoulders' invisible plunge; it would not glisten like the fur of some wild animal; it would not burst forth from its marble confines like a star; for there is no way—no way whatever—that you can escape its penetrating gaze. You must change your life. (*New Poems* 2–3; our translation)

In these lines, Rilke describes a mental transformation analogous to the one to which Perelman and Olbrechts-Tyteca allude when they speak about presence as a psychological phenomenon: "Accordingly one of the preoccupations of the speaker is to make present, by verbal magic alone, what is actually absent but what he considers important to his argument or, by making them more present, to enhance the value of some of the elements of which one has actually been made conscious" (117). Rilke represents this transformation by means of metaphors of light and animation, coupled with a shift in the use of pronouns. He starts in the third person – he is visiting the sculpture gallery with the reader – but he soon switches to the second person familiar, a tense of intimacy, an effect not possible in English. This is the note of intimacy on which the poem ends: "*Du* musst dein Leben ändern" (emphasis added).

There is no transition to this final, startling half-line; it is simply that a point has been reached at which our impressions of the statue are such that qualitative change suddenly supervenes, a point at which perception becomes illumination. It is not only, as Perelman and Olbrechts-Tyteca say, that presence fills "the whole field of consciousness" (118); it is also that presence transforms that consciousness; it alters our world. The effect is psychological and argumentative, yes; but not merely psychological and argumentative; it is also, in our view, existential.

Speakers and writers whose purpose is persuasion aspire to a like transformation on the part of their audiences. Douglas hopes that the auditor will accept as real a racist and imperial America; Descartes hopes that the reader will accept as real the need for a fundamental reconstruction of philosophy; Fitzpatrick and his co-authors hope that their readers accept as real a new species of hummingbird. In each case, to be persuaded is to live a world made significantly different by the persuader.

Conclusion

We may summarize by saying that presence is most interestingly considered as a second-order effect, an effect of synergy. Although initially psychological in nature, presence becomes an element in argumentation because its primary effect, constructing and reconstructing the reality speakers hope to share with their audiences, inevitably affects adherence. Presence is a fact, not only in argument in the public sphere, but also in argument in philosophy and science, though naturally in the latter two cases the devices of presence are constrained by the need to reach a universal audience. Presence does not undermine rational theories of argumentation, such as that of Perelman and Olbrechts-Tyteca, because such theories found rationality not on argument as an artifact, but on arguing as a process. No argument is rational in itself; arguments are redeemed rationally by means of speakers' interaction with their audiences in appropriate forums. Finally, despite Perelman and Olbrechts-Tyteca's disavowal, the presence they identify creates a rhetorical reality with existential implications.

Notes

Chapter 1. Perelman's Life and Influence

1. According to Perelman's daughter, Noémi Mattis-Perelman, her father's Polish given name at birth was Henio (Henri in French), the phonetic analogue of which is Chaim in Hebrew. Perelman is said to have adopted the name Chaim following World War II in honor of Chaim Weizman, the first president of Israel (Mattis *Tzedek* 5). This account is corroborated by Perelman's close friend, Mieczyslaw Maneli (35). It is an historical fact, however, that although he was called Henri as a youngster, Perelman's first publications during his undergraduate years at Brussels, written in the early thirties, appeared under the name of "Chaim," sometimes abbreviated "Ch." (see "Esquisse," "A Propos," "Le Statut Social," "De l'Arbitraire"). It should be added that the name Henri is not found in the biographical entries for Perelman in the standard reference works. Nor does it appear in the memoirs of the Belgian resistance leaders who have written about Perelman's exploits during the Occupation. To complicate matters, a 1954 article ("Proof in Philosophy," *Hibbert Journal*) appears under the name of "Charles Perelman." Since Perelman usually abbreviated his first name, this anomaly probably resulted from an editorial misunderstanding, a conjecture offered by Noémi Mattis-Perelman in an interview with David Frank in June, 1999.
2. Perelman assumed that Johnstone had been the prime mover behind the invitation, and the tone of Oliver's 1963 piece in *Logique et Analyse* lends weight to that assumption. See "The New Rhetoric and the Rhetoricians," 189, and Oliver "Philosophy and/or Persuasion," 572.
3. These are our translated titles of works published in French by Bruylant in Brussels.

Chapter 3. A Theory of the Rhetorical Audience

1. Epideictic is the genre of oratory most centrally concerned with values. This is a genre that Perelman and Olbrechts-Tyteca think has been seriously misunderstood, a misconception stemming from Aristotle's view that the primary criterion for judging such discourse is aesthetic. For this reason, it is often

called ceremonial discourse. The Belgians think that nothing could be further from the truth. For them, an epideictic discourse is not peripheral, but rather "forms a central part of the art of persuasion" (49). It is designed "to strengthen the disposition toward action by increasing adherence to the values it lauds" (50).

2. Although elsewhere in the *Phaedrus*, Socrates makes extensive use of imaginative allegory, his "flights of fancy" are always under strict intellectual control.

Chapter 7. Rhetoric as a Technique and a Mode of Truth

1. We take Warnick's suggestion that Perelman is responsible for the philosophical content of his joint work with Olbrechts-Tyteca.
2. Of course, as Kenneth Burke points out, both of Antony's audiences, the Roman mob and the theatrical audience, are being manipulated, though in very different ways. To his theatrical audience, Antony's speech unironically reveals a vengeful purpose, a desire to unleash "the dogs of war" against the conspirators (3.1.273). But this does not mean that Antony is entirely free from guile with an audience that has just become unwitting co-conspirators in an assassination. Addressing the theatrical audience in a soliloquy now entirely of Burke's own devising, Antony says: "You have been made conspirators in a murder. For this transgression, there must be some expiative beast brought up for sacrifice. Such requirements guide us in the mixing of the Brutus recipe, for it is Brutus that must die to absolve you . . ." (334). According to Burke, the ground is laid for this sacrifice by showing that Brutus breaks the bonds of friendship and that the conspirators brush aside the obligations of hospitality. In this way, Burke says, Shakespeare dissociates their actions from the course of justice (336–337). In this sense, the funeral oration is doubly manipulative, each manipulation being coincident with the same political purpose on Shakespeare's part: the absolute condemnation of political murder.
3. All interpretations of this speech are indebted to Leff and Mohrmann's classical and cogent analysis.
4. This interpretation of the *Phaedrus* is heavily indebted to that of Nehamas and Woodruff in "Plato."
5. These matters are of course contingent. In the United States, the additional coherence of private and public selves seems to be emerging as a political imperative.

Chapter 9. The Figures as Argument

1. For the interesting comments of the Belgians on style generally, see *The New Rhetoric*, 149–167.
2. As Ortony's volume makes clear, any statement about metaphor is bound to

be controversial. We say only in this instance that our claim is consistent with the Belgians' and defensible.

3. We take no responsibility for Lincoln's wayward syntax in this last sentence.
4. One of the authors thanks his student, Doreen Stärke-Meyerring, for having made this point about this passage.
5. This view is subject to contention. See Boyd in Ortony.

Bibliography

Works by Chaim Perelman

Books

Le Champ de l'Argumentation. Brussels: Presses Universitaires de Bruxelles, 1970.

From Metaphysics to Rhetoric. Michel Meyer, ed. Robert Harvey, tr. Dordrecht: Kluwer, 1989.

An Historical Introduction to Philosophical Thinking. Kenneth A. Brown, tr. New York: Random House, 1965.

The Idea of Justice and the Problem of Argument. John Petrie, tr. New York: Humanities Press, 1963.

Justice. New York: Random House, 1967.

Justice, Law, and Argument: Essays on Moral and Legal Reasoning. John Petrie et al., tr. Dordrecht: D. Reidel, 1980.

Logique Juridique, Nouvelle Rhétorique. Paris: Dalloz, 1976.

The New Rhetoric: A Treatise on Argumentation. John Wilkinson and Purcell Weaver, tr. Notre Dame: University of Notre Dame Press, 1969.

The New Rhetoric and the Humanities: Essays on Rhetoric and Its Applications. Boston: D. Reidel, 1979.

The Realm of Rhetoric. William Kluback. tr. Notre Dame: University of Notre Dame Press, 1982.

Rhétorique et Philosophie: Pour une Théorie de l'Argumentation en Philosophie. Paris: Presses Universitaires de France, 1952.

Articles

"Act and Person in Argument." *Ethics* 61 (July, 1951): 251–269. (with L. Olbrechts-Tyteca)

"Une Conception de la Philosophie." *Revue de l'Institut de Sociologie* 20 (1940): 39–50.

"De l'Arbitraire dans la Connaissance." *Archives de la Societé Belge de Philosophie* (Brussels, 1933). 44 pages.

"Esquisse d'une Logistique des Valeurs." *Revue de l'Université de Bruxelles* (1931): 486–496.

"How Do We Apply Reason to Values?" *Journal of Philosophy* 52 (December 22, 1955): 797–802.

Interview. Hotel King David, March 20, 1964. New York Times Oral History Program. Hebrew University. Contemporary Jewry Oral History Collection. Part II—World War II. Holocaust Resistance and Rescue No. 231. Glen Rock, NJ: Microfilming Corporation of America, 1975.

"Logique et Rhétorique." *Revue Philosophique* 140 (January, 1950): 1–35. (with L. Olbrechts-Tyteca)

"The New Rhetoric." In Lloyd F. Bitzer and Edwin Black, eds. *The Prospect of Rhetoric*. Englewood Cliffs, NJ: Prentice-Hall, 1971. Pages 115–122.

"The New Rhetoric." Francis B. Sullivan, tr. *Philosophy Today* 1 (March, 1957): 4–10. (with L. Olbrechts-Tyteca)

"The New Rhetoric and the Rhetoricians." Ray D. Dearin, tr. *Quarterly Journal of Speech* 70 (1984): 188–196.

"Old and New Rhetoric." In James L. Golden, Goodwin F. Berquist, and William E. Coleman, eds. *The Rhetoric of Western Thought*. 6th ed. Dubuque: Kendall/Hunt, 1997.

"On Self-Evidence in Metaphysics." *International Philosophical Quarterly* 4 (February, 1964): 5–19.

"Philosophies Premières et Philosophie Régressive." *Dialectica* 3 (1949): 175–191.

"Philosophy and Rhetoric." In J. Robert Cox and Charles Arthur Willard, eds. *Advances in Argumentation Theory and Research*. Carbondale: Southern Illinois University Press, 1982. Pages 287–297.

"Polanyi's Interpretation of Scientific Inquiry." Thomas A. Langford and William H. Poteat, eds. Donald W. Millholland, tr. *Intellect and Hope: Essays in the Thought of Michael Polanyi*. Durham, NC: Duke University Press, 1968. Pages 232–241.

Preface to *Introduction à la Logique Juridique*. By Georges Kalinowski. Paris: Librarie Générale de Droit et de Jurisprudence, 1965.

"Proof in Philosophy." *Hibbert Journal* 52 (July, 1954): 354–359.

"A Propos de la Philosophie de M. Dupréel." *Revue de l'Université de Bruxelles* (1932): 385–399.

"Réflexions sur la Justice." *Revue de l'Institut de Sociologie* 24 (1951): 255–281.

"Reply to Henry W. Johnstone, Jr." In Maurice Natanson and Henry Johnstone, eds. *Philosophy, Rhetoric and Argumentation*. University Park, PA: The Pennsylvania State University Press, 1965. Pages 135–137.

"Rhetoric and Philosophy." Henry W. Johnstone, Jr, tr. *Philosophy and Rhetoric* 1 (January, 1968): 15–24.

"Rhetoric and Politics." *Philosophy and Rhetoric* 17 (1984): 129–134.

"Sociologie de la Connaissance et Philosophie de la Connaissance." *Revue Internationale de Philosophie* 4 (July, 1950): 309–317.
"Le Statut Social des Jugements de Vérité." *Revue de l'Institut de Sociologie* 13 (1933): 17–23.
"The Use and Abuse of Confused Notions." *ETC.: A Review of General Semantics* 36 (1979): 313–324.
"Value Judgments, Justifications and Argumentation." Francis B. Sullivan, tr. *Philosophy Today* 6 (Spring, 1962): 45–50.

Works about Perelman

Arnold, Caroll. "Perelman's New Rhetoric." *Quarterly Journal of Speech* 55 (1970): 87–92.
Costello, H. T. Review of Perelman's "De l'Arbitraire dans la Connaissance." *Journal of Philosophy* 31 (October 25, 1934): 613.
Dearin, Ray D. "Chaim Perelman's Theory of Rhetoric." Ph.D. dissertation. University of Illinois, 1970.
Dearin, Ray. "The Philosophical Basis of Chaim Perelman's Theory of Rhetoric." *Quarterly Journal of Speech* 55 (1969): 213–224.
———, ed. *The New Rhetoric of Chaim Perelman: Statement and Response*. Lanham, MD: University Press of America, 1989.
Frank, David A. "The New Rhetoric, Judaism, and Post-Enlightenment Thought: The Cultural Origins of Perelmanian Philosophy." *Quarterly Journal of Speech* 83 (1997): 311–331.
Ede, Lisa S. "Rhetoric Versus Philosophy: The Role of the Universal Audience in Chaim Perelman's *The New Rheoric*." In Dearin, ed., *The New Rhetoric of Chaim Perelman*, pp. 141–151.
Gross, Alan G. *The Rhetoric of Science*. Cambridge: Harvard University Press, 1996.
Golden, James L. "The Universal Audience Revisited." In James L. Golden and Joseph J. Pilotta, eds., *Practical Reasoning in Human Affairs: Studies in Honor of Chaim Perelman*. Dordrecht: D. Reidel, 1986. Pages 287–304.
Johnstone, Henry W., Jr. "New Outlooks on Controversy." In *Validity and Rhetoric in Philosophical Argument: An Oulook in Transition*. University Park, PA: The Dialogue Press of Man & World, 1978. Pages 93–100.
Karon, Louise. "Presence in *The New Rhetoric*." In Ray D. Dearin, ed. *The New Rhetoric of Chaim Perelman: Statement and Response*, pages 163–178.
Mattis, Noémi Perelman. "Perelman and Olbrechts-Tyteca: A Personal Recollection." Unpublished letter to Ray D. Dearin. August 11, 1994.
———. Interview with David Frank. Salt Lake City, Utah. February 4, 1994. In David Frank, "*Tzedek Tzedek Tirdof*: Perelman, Judaism, and the New Rhetoric."

Paper presented at the Speech Communication Association annual conference. New Orleans, Louisiana. November 20, 1994.
Measell, James S. "Perelman on Analogy." *Journal of the American Forensics Association* 22 (1985): 65–71.
Murphy, John M. "Presence, Analogy, and *Earth in the Balance*." *Argument and Advocacy* 31 (1994): 1–16.
Oliver, Robert T. "Philosophy and/or Persuasion." *Logique et Analyse* 6 (1983): 571–580.
Ray, John W. "Perelman's Universal Audience." *Quarterly Journal of Speech* 64 (1978): 361–375.
Wallace, Karl R. "Topoi and the Problem of Invention." *Quarterly Journal of Speech* 58 (1972): 387–395.
Warnick, Barbara. "Lucie Olbrechts-Tyteca's Contribution to *The New Rhetoric*." In Molly Meijer Wertheimer, ed. *Listening to Their Voices: The Rhetorical Activities of Historical Women*. Columbia: University of South Carolina Press, 1997. Pages 69–85.

Other Works

Aristotle. *Ethica Nicomachea*. W. D. Ross, tr. *The Basic Works of Aristotle*. Richard McKeon, ed. New York: Random House, 1941.
Aristotle. *On Rhetoric: A Theory of Civic Discourse*. George Kennedy, tr. Oxford: Oxford University Press, 1991.
———. *Rhetoric*. W. Rhys Roberts, tr. *The Rhetoric and Poetics of Aristotle*. New York: The Modern Library, 1954.
Bacon, Francis. *The Advancement of Learning*. G. W. Kitchin, ed. London: Dent, 1962.
———. *Essays, Advancement of Learning, New Atlantis, and Other Pieces*. Richard Foster Jones, ed. New York: Odyssey Press, 1937.
Baird, A. Craig. *American Public Addresses 1740–1952*. New York: McGraw-Hill, 1956.
Boyd, Richard. "Metaphor and Theory Change: What Is 'Metaphor' a Metaphor For?" In Ortony, ed. *Metaphor and Thought*, pages 481–532.
Brody, Stuart, and Charles Yanofsky. "Suppressor Gene Alteration of Primary Protein Structure." Reprinted in Herbert J. Taylor, ed. *Selected Papers on Molecular Genetics*. New York: Academic Press, 1965. Pages 634–641.
Burke, Kenneth. *A Grammar of Motives*. New York: Prentice-Hall, 1945.
———. "Antony on Behalf of the Play." In *The Philosophy of Literary Form: Studies in Symbolic Action*. 2nd ed. Baton Rouge: Louisiana State University Press, 1967. Pages 329–343.
———. "Four Master Tropes." In *A Grammar of Motives*, pages 503–517.

Campbell, George. *The Philosophy of Rhetoric*. Lloyd F. Bitzer, ed. Carbondale: Southern Illinois Press, 1963.

Carpenter, Ronald H. "General Douglas MacArthur's Oratory on Behalf of Inchon: Discourse that Altered the Course of History." *The Southern Communication Journal* 58 (1992): 1–12.

Churchill, Winston S. *Winston S. Churchill: His Complete Speeches*. 8 vols. Robert Rhodes James, ed. New York and London: Chelsea House Publishers, 1974.

Cicero. *Nine Orations and the Dream of Scipio*. Palmer Bovie, tr. New York: Mentor, 1967.

Cicero. *The Verrine Orations*, II. L. G. H. Greenwood, ed. Cambridge: Harvard University Press, 1988.

"Clinton Charts the Next 4 Years." *Des Moines Register*. August 30, 1996: 21A.

Corbett, Edward P. J. *Classical Rhetoric for the Modern Student*. 3rd ed. New York: Oxford University Press, 1990.

Crick, F. H. C., Leslie Barnett, S. Brenner, and R. J. Watts-Tobin. "General Nature of the Genetic Code for Proteins." *Nature* 192 (1961): 1227–1232.

——, J. S. Griffin, and L. E. Orgel. "Codes without Commas." *Proceedings of the National Academy of Sciences* 43 (1957): 416.

Darwin, Charles. *The Origin of Species by Means of Natural Selection or the Preservation of Favoured Races in the Struggle for Life*. New York: Collier Books, 1978 [6th ed. 1872].

Descartes, René. *Discourse on Method* and *Meditations*. F. E. Sutcliffe. tr. London: Penguin Books, 1968.

Dicker, George. *Descartes: An Analytical and Historical Introduction*. New York: Oxford University Press, 1993.

Dole, Bob. "Remarks Prepared for Delivery, Republican Candidate for President of the United States, Republican National Convention, San Diego, California, Thursday, August 15, 1996." Press release text.

Dupréel, Eugène. *Traité de Morale*. Brussels: Editions de la Revue de l'Université de Bruxelles, 1932.

"Earl Spencer's Funeral Address." http//:homepages.tcp.co.uk/~nicholson/diana.html

Einstein, Albert. *Ideas and Opinions*. New York: Bonanza Books, 1954. Quoted passage originally published in *Freedom, Its Meaning*. Ruth Nanda Anshon, ed. New York: Harcourt, Brace and Co., 1940.

——. *Relativity: The Special and General Theory*. Tr. Robert W. Lawson. New York: Crown Publishers, 1961.

Foss, Sonja K., Karen Foss, and Robert Trapp. *Contemporary Perspectives on Rhetoric*. 2nd ed. Prospect Heights, IL: Waveland, 1991.

Franklin, Benjamin. *A Benjamin Franklin Reader*. Nathan G. Goodman, ed. New York: Thomas Y. Crowell Company, 1945.

Gérard-Libois, Jules, and José Gotovich. *L'An 40: La Belgique Occupée*. Brussels: Crisp, n.d.

Habermas, Jürgen. *Between Facts and Norms: Contributions to a Discourse Theory of Law and Democracy*. Tr. William Rehg. Cambridge: MIT Press, 1998.

Harris, Robert. "A Handbook of Rhetorical Devices." 19 August 1997. Online. 11 August 1998. http://www.sccu.edu/faculty/R_Harris/rhetoric.htm

Hart, H. L. A. *The Concept of Law*. Oxford: The Clarendon Press, 1961.

Kauffman, Charles, and Donn W. Parson, "Metaphor and Presence in Argument." In David Cratis Williams and Michael David Hazen, eds. *Argument Theory and the Rhetoric of Assent*. Tuscaloosa: University of Alabama Press, 1990. Pages 91–102.

King, Jr., Martin Luther. *I Have a Dream: Writings and Speeches that Changed the World*. James Melvin Washington, ed. San Francisco: Harper, 1992.

Lanham, Richard. *A Handlist of Rhetorical Terms: A Guide for Students of English Literature*. Berkeley: University of California Press, 1969.

Latour, Bruno, and Steve Woolgar. *Laboratory Life: The Construction of Scientific Facts*. Princeton: Princeton University Press, 1986.

Leff, Michael C., and Gerald P. Mohrmann. "Lincoln at Cooper Union: A Rhetorical Analysis of the Text." *Quarterly Journal of Speech* 60 (1974): 346–358.

Lewis, Clarence Irving. *An Analysis of Knowledge and Valuation*. La Salle, IL: Open Court Publishing Co, 1946.

Lincoln, Abraham. *Abraham Lincoln: His Speeches and Writings*. Roy P. Basler, ed. New York: Da Capo Press, 1946.

The Lincoln-Douglas Debates: The First Complete, Unexpurgated Text. Harold Holzer, ed. New York: HarperCollins, 1994.

Loreau, Max. "Rhetoric as the Logic of the Behavioral Sciences." Lloyd I. Watkins and Paul D. Brandes, tr. *Quarterly Journal of Speech* 51 (1965): 455–463.

Maneli, Mieczyslaw. "The New Rhetoric and Dialectics." *Revue Internationale de Philosophie* (1979): 216–238.

———. "Perelman's Achievement Beyond Traditional Philosophy and Politics." *Law and Philosophy* 5 (1986): 351–367.

———. *Perelman's New Rhetoric as Philosophy and Methodology for the Next Century*. Boston: Kluwer, 1994.

Mohrmann, G. P, and Michael C. Leff. "Lincoln at the Cooper Union: A Rationale for Neo-Classical Criticism." *Quarterly Journal of Speech* 60 (1974): 459–467.

The New Analytical Bible and Dictionary of the Bible. Authorized King James Version. Chicago: John A. Dickinson Publishing Co., 1950.

Nirenberg, Marshall W., and J. Henry Matthaei. "The Dependence of Cell-Free Protein Synthesis in *E. Coli* upon Naturally Occurring or Synthetic Polyribonucleotides." *Proceedings of the National Academy of Sciences* 47 (1961): 1588–1602.

Olbrechts-Tyteca, L. "Rencontre avec la Rhétorique." *Logique et Analyse* 6 (1963): 3–18.

Oliver, Robert T. "The Way It Was—All the Way." *Communication Quarterly* 45 (1997): 2–130.

Ortony, Andrew, ed. *Metaphor and* Thought. 2nd. ed. Cambridge: Cambridge University Press, 1993.

Pearson, Allison. In the *Evening Standard.* Cited in the Pittsburgh *Post-Gazette*, November 28, 1997, p. A-9.

Plato. *Phaedrus*. Alexander Nehamas and Paul Woodruff, ed. and tr. Indianapolis: Hackett, 1995.

Ptolemy, Claudius. *Ptolemy's Almagest*, G. J. Toomer, tr. New York: Springer Verlag, 1984.

Reid, Ronald F. *American Rhetorical Discourse*. 2nd ed. Prospect Heights, IL: Waveland Press, 1995.

Richards, I. A. *The Philosophy of Rhetoric.* New York: Oxford University Press, 1965.

Rilke, Rainer Maria. "Archaïscher Torso Apollos." In *New Poems: The Other Part.* Edward Snow, tr. San Francisco: North Point Press, 1987. Pages 2–3.

Rorty, Amélie Okensberg. "The Structure of Descartes's *Meditations*." In Amélie Okensberg Rorty, ed. *Essays on Descartes's* Meditations. Princeton: Princeton University Press, 1980. Pages 1–20.

Rosteck, Thomas. "Narrative in Martin Luther King's *I've Been to the Mountaintop*." *The Southern Communication Journal* 58 (Fall, 1992): 22–32.

Ryan, Halford Ross. *Contemporary American Public Discourse*. 3rd ed. Prospect Heights, IL: Waveland Press, 1992.

Sandburg, Carl. *Abraham Lincoln: The War Years*. 4 vols. New York: Harcourt, Brace, and Company, 1939.

Schrödinger, Erwin. *What Is Life? The Physical Aspect of the Living Cell.* Cambridge: Cambridge University Press, 1967.

Scult, Allen. "Perelman's Universal Audience: One Perspective." In Dearin, *The New Rhetoric*, pages 153–162.

Shakespeare, William. *Julius Caesar*. Marvin Spevack, ed. Cambridge: Cambridge University Press, 1988.

Steinberg, Maxime. *L'Étoile et le Fusil: La Traque des Juifs*, 1942–1944. Vols. 1 and 2. Brussels: Vie Ouvrière, 1983.

Stone, Julius. *Human Law and Human Justice*. Stanford, CA: Stanford University Press, 1965.

_____. *Legal System and Lawyers' Reasonings*. Stanford, CA: Stanford University Press, 1964.

Swales, John. 1990. *Genre Analysis: English in Academic and Research Settings*. Cambridge: Cambridge University Press, 1990.

Toulmin, Stephen Edelston. *The Uses of Argument*. Cambridge: Cambridge University Press, 1958.

van Eemeren, F. H., R. Grootendorst, and T. Kruiger. *The Study of Argumentation.* New York: Irvington Publishers, 1984.

Watson, J. D., and F. H. C. Crick. "A Structure for Deoxyribose Nucleic Acid." *Nature* 171 (1953): 737–738.

The World's Most Famous Court Trial: Tennessee Evolution Case. Cincinnati: National Book Company, 1925.

Zarefsky, David. *Lincoln, Douglas, and Slavery: In the Crucible of Public Debate.* Chicago: University of Chicago Press, 1990.

Zillmann, Dolf, and Hans-Bernd Brosius. *Exemplification in Communication: The Influence of Case Reports on the Perception of Issues.* Mahwah, NJ: Erlbaum Associates, 2000.

Zyskind, H. "The New Rhetoric and Formalism." *Revue Internationale de Philosophie* (1979): 18–32.

Index

Books in the Rhetoric in the Modern Era Series

Chaim Perelman
Alan G. Gross and Ray D. Dearin

Adam Smith: The Rhetoric of Propriety
Stephen J. McKenna

Paul Ricoeur: Tradition and Innovation in Rhetorical Theory
Andreea Deciu Ritivoi

George Campbell: Rhetoric in the Age of Enlightenment
Arthur E. Walzer